Vulnerability Management in Practice

James Relington

DEDICATION

To those who seek knowledge, inspiration, and new perspectives—
may this book be a companion on your journey, a spark for curiosity,
and a reminder that every page turned is a step toward discovery.

AKNOWLEDGEMENTS

I would like to express my deepest gratitude to everyone who contributed to the creation of this book. To my colleagues and mentors, your insights and expertise have been invaluable. A special thank you to my family and friends for their unwavering support and encouragement throughout this journey.

Understanding the Threat Landscape

Understanding the threat landscape is the foundational step in building an effective vulnerability management program. Without a clear and continuously evolving grasp of the environment in which vulnerabilities exist, it is nearly impossible to make informed decisions regarding risk prioritization, resource allocation, and mitigation strategies. The term "threat landscape" encompasses the wide array of potential actors, tools, techniques, and procedures that pose risks to an organization's digital infrastructure. It includes not only the technical components of cyber threats but also the geopolitical, social, and economic factors that influence the behavior of threat actors.

The modern threat landscape is highly dynamic. New vulnerabilities are discovered daily, and threat actors are constantly refining their methods to exploit weaknesses in systems, software, and even people. Attackers range from opportunistic hackers and criminal syndicates to state-sponsored groups with access to sophisticated tools and nearly unlimited resources. Their motivations can include financial gain, political agendas, corporate espionage, or simply the challenge of breaking into secure environments. As their methods become more advanced, so too must the defenses and awareness of security professionals tasked with protecting systems and data.

One of the key aspects of understanding the threat landscape is identifying the types of threats most relevant to a particular organization. This includes recognizing industry-specific risks. For example, a financial institution may face more advanced persistent threats (APTs) targeting customer data and financial assets, while a manufacturing company might encounter attacks focused on disrupting operational technology and supply chains. Similarly, healthcare organizations face constant threats to patient records and critical medical systems. Each sector has unique attack surfaces, and understanding these nuances is essential to formulating effective defense strategies.

It is also important to examine the evolution of threats over time. In the early days of the internet, threats were often the work of individual hackers seeking notoriety or testing their skills. Over time, these efforts gave way to organized cybercrime, where groups began exploiting vulnerabilities for financial gain. Ransomware emerged as a dominant threat, encrypting critical systems and demanding payment in cryptocurrencies for their release. Today, ransomware-as-a-service allows less technically skilled criminals to launch attacks using prebuilt tools developed by more sophisticated actors. This commoditization of cyber threats means that a broader array of actors can cause significant damage with minimal effort or expertise.

The proliferation of connected devices and cloud-based services has further expanded the attack surface. With the rise of remote work and the Internet of Things, organizations must now account for vulnerabilities not only within their internal networks but also across a wide array of endpoints and third-party services. Each new device or integration introduces potential weaknesses, and attackers are quick to exploit any gaps in security posture. Understanding the implications of this expanded landscape requires constant vigilance, real-time intelligence, and cross-functional collaboration between security, IT, and business units.

Threat intelligence plays a critical role in understanding and navigating the threat landscape. It involves gathering data from internal logs, external threat feeds, industry reports, dark web monitoring, and information sharing groups. By analyzing patterns of attack and identifying emerging threats, organizations can proactively adjust their vulnerability management strategies. For instance, if a specific vulnerability is being actively exploited in the wild, it should be prioritized for remediation even if its severity score is not the highest. Context is key, and real-time intelligence provides that context.

Another vital component is the human factor. Social engineering, phishing, and insider threats remain among the most effective means of compromise. While technical vulnerabilities in software and hardware are crucial to address, they are often exploited in conjunction with manipulation of human behavior. Employees can be tricked into disclosing credentials, clicking malicious links, or installing harmful software. Understanding the threat landscape, therefore, requires not only a technical lens but also a psychological and behavioral perspective. Security awareness training, clear policies, and strong internal communication can help mitigate these human-centric threats.

Moreover, the threat landscape is shaped by broader global events. Geopolitical tensions, conflicts, pandemics, and economic instability can all influence the frequency and nature of cyberattacks. During times of political unrest or global crisis, there is often a surge in cyber activity as threat actors seek to exploit distraction, confusion, or weakened defenses. For example, during the COVID-19 pandemic, there was a notable increase in phishing campaigns related to health information, as well as attacks targeting remote access systems. Being aware of global trends and their potential security implications is an essential part of understanding the broader threat environment.

Effective vulnerability management begins with this holistic understanding. Organizations must move beyond reactive models and embrace a proactive approach grounded in continuous situational awareness. This includes staying informed through threat intelligence platforms, participating in information sharing communities, and regularly reviewing and updating risk assessments. As threats evolve, so too must the mindset and tools used to combat them. No organization operates in a vacuum, and the interconnectedness of today's digital world means that vulnerabilities in one part of the ecosystem can have ripple effects across industries and regions.

Ultimately, understanding the threat landscape is not a one-time effort but an ongoing commitment. It requires curiosity, adaptability, and a willingness to challenge assumptions. By staying attuned to the shifting contours of cyber threats and maintaining a vigilant posture, organizations can position themselves to respond more effectively to vulnerabilities, reduce risk, and build resilience in an increasingly hostile digital environment.

The Lifecycle of a Vulnerability

The lifecycle of a vulnerability is a continuous and complex journey that begins with the introduction of a flaw in a system and often ends long after it is patched or exploited. Understanding this lifecycle is crucial for any organization seeking to build a resilient vulnerability management program. It is not enough to simply react when a vulnerability is disclosed. Instead, security teams must anticipate the stages through which a vulnerability evolves, monitor its progression, and take proactive measures to mitigate its potential impact.

The origin of a vulnerability typically starts during the development phase of software or hardware. Whether due to coding errors, logic flaws, misconfigurations, or design oversights, vulnerabilities are almost always unintentional. In many cases, they arise from the pressure to deliver features quickly, which can lead developers to take shortcuts or miss subtle issues during testing. Secure coding practices, code reviews, and automated testing tools can help reduce the number of vulnerabilities introduced, but no system is ever completely free of flaws. Even the most mature development pipelines are susceptible to human error and evolving technical complexities.

Once a vulnerability exists within a system, it often remains unknown for some time. This latent period can last days, months, or even years, depending on the type of vulnerability, its location within the system, and the attention it receives from researchers or attackers. During this dormant phase, the vulnerability poses a risk simply by existing, though it has not yet been identified or disclosed. If discovered by a security researcher or a responsible entity, the vulnerability may enter a coordinated disclosure process. In contrast, if discovered by a malicious actor, it may become an instrument of exploitation long before anyone else is aware of its presence.

When a vulnerability is identified, it begins to move through a phase of assessment and verification. Security researchers or internal teams validate its existence, understand its potential impact, and determine how it might be exploited. This process is critical because not all discovered flaws represent actual risks. Some may be theoretical or require highly specific conditions to be exploited. This is also when security professionals assign severity ratings using systems like the Common Vulnerability Scoring System (CVSS), helping organizations prioritize their responses based on a mix of technical and business factors.

If the vulnerability is disclosed publicly or through coordinated efforts, vendors and developers are typically notified. This stage marks a critical inflection point in the lifecycle, as the clock starts ticking on remediation. Vendors must investigate the flaw, understand its root cause, and develop a patch or workaround. Depending on the complexity of the system and the resources available, this process can vary in length. In open-source environments, community collaboration may accelerate the process, while proprietary systems may take longer due to internal constraints or bureaucratic delays. The speed and quality of the patch are vital because any delay in remediation increases the window of opportunity for attackers.

Once a patch is developed, it must be tested and deployed. This phase, often underestimated, is fraught with challenges. Organizations must balance the urgency of fixing a known issue with the need to maintain system stability and operational continuity. Patching can introduce new bugs, disrupt dependencies, or conflict with existing configurations. For this reason, many organizations adopt staged deployment strategies, testing patches in development or staging environments before rolling them out to production. The longer this process takes, however, the greater the risk, especially if proof-of-concept code or active exploits are already in circulation.

Meanwhile, threat actors are monitoring public disclosures and vulnerability databases just as closely as defenders. Once a vulnerability becomes known, attackers often rush to weaponize it.

They may develop exploit code, incorporate it into automated attack tools, or sell it on underground markets. In some cases, vulnerabilities are exploited within hours of disclosure, especially if the attack vector is simple and the impact is high. This race between attackers and defenders underscores the importance of speed and coordination in the vulnerability lifecycle. The faster an organization can assess, test, and apply a patch, the lower its exposure to exploitation.

Even after a vulnerability is patched, its lifecycle does not necessarily end. Legacy systems, unpatched endpoints, and forgotten applications can remain vulnerable for extended periods. Attackers often revisit old vulnerabilities in the hope of finding systems that have been neglected or misconfigured. This is why vulnerability management is not a one-time task but a continuous process. Regular scanning, inventory tracking, and compliance auditing are essential to ensure that patches are applied universally and that no remnants of a vulnerability remain in the environment.

Moreover, the lifecycle of a vulnerability can take on new dimensions when it intersects with other issues. A seemingly low-risk vulnerability might be chained with others to form a more serious attack vector. Similarly, changes in the threat landscape, such as the discovery of a new exploit technique or the rise of a specific attack group, can elevate the importance of an old vulnerability. Security professionals must remain vigilant, not only tracking the technical status of a vulnerability but also contextualizing it within the broader environment in which it exists.

Vulnerability lifecycles also generate data that can be used to refine and improve security practices. By analyzing the time it takes to detect, disclose, patch, and remediate vulnerabilities, organizations can identify bottlenecks and inefficiencies in their processes. Metrics such as mean time to remediation (MTTR) and patch adoption rates provide insight into operational readiness and responsiveness. Over time, these insights can inform policy changes, investment decisions, and training priorities, ultimately enhancing the organization's overall security posture.

In sum, the lifecycle of a vulnerability is not a linear path but a series of evolving stages influenced by discovery methods, disclosure practices, patching capabilities, and adversarial activity. Each stage presents unique challenges and requires timely, informed decision-making. By understanding the full scope of this lifecycle, security teams can more effectively anticipate threats, reduce risk, and build a culture of proactive vulnerability management that evolves alongside the systems it protects.

Risk-Based Vulnerability Management

Risk-based vulnerability management represents a shift from traditional, one-size-fits-all approaches to a more strategic and context-aware methodology. It is a recognition that not all vulnerabilities pose the same level of threat to an organization and that resources are often limited. Therefore, prioritizing efforts based on the actual risk each vulnerability presents becomes essential. This model is designed to reduce the noise that can overwhelm security teams and focus attention where it matters most, aligning remediation activities with business objectives and operational realities.

The foundation of risk-based vulnerability management lies in understanding that risk is a function of several interconnected factors. These include the severity of the vulnerability itself, the criticality of the affected asset, the exposure of that asset to potential attackers, the likelihood of exploitation, and the potential business impact if the vulnerability were to be successfully exploited. By assessing and weighing these elements together, organizations can make more intelligent decisions about which vulnerabilities to remediate first and which ones can be monitored or temporarily accepted as part of a broader risk posture.

One of the key benefits of this approach is its ability to bridge the gap between technical assessments and business risk. Traditional vulnerability management often focuses purely on technical severity scores, such as those provided by the Common Vulnerability Scoring System (CVSS). While these scores provide valuable insight into the potential impact of a vulnerability in isolation, they do not account for the context in which the vulnerability exists. A critical CVSS score might suggest an urgent issue, but if the system is isolated from the internet, not connected to sensitive data, and protected by multiple layers of defense, the real-world risk may be minimal. Conversely, a medium-severity vulnerability in a mission-critical system with high exposure could represent a much more serious threat.

To implement a risk-based approach effectively, organizations must have visibility into their assets and understand their value and function within the business. Asset inventory and classification become critical components of the process. Each asset must be mapped according to its sensitivity, its role in daily operations, and its exposure to internal and external threats. This allows security teams to associate vulnerabilities with business impact, ensuring that risk is evaluated not only in technical terms but also in the context of organizational priorities.

Another vital element of this strategy is threat intelligence. Real-time insights into active exploit campaigns, attacker behavior, and evolving tactics can dramatically shift the risk profile of a given vulnerability. A vulnerability that is not currently being exploited may carry a lower priority, but if threat intelligence reveals that it is being actively targeted in the wild, its risk level must be reevaluated. Integrating this intelligence into the vulnerability management workflow enables dynamic, informed decisions rather than relying on static data alone. This responsiveness is key to staying ahead of adversaries who constantly adapt to changing defenses.

Automation plays a crucial role in scaling risk-based vulnerability management. With thousands of vulnerabilities disclosed each year and large, complex environments to protect, manual risk assessments are no longer viable. Organizations increasingly rely on tools that aggregate asset data, correlate vulnerabilities with threat intelligence, and apply risk-scoring algorithms to prioritize remediation efforts. These systems help reduce the burden on security teams by cutting through the volume of alerts and presenting a more focused list of high-risk issues that require immediate attention. However, automation must be complemented by human oversight to ensure contextual accuracy and alignment with business objectives.

Communication between departments is another critical factor. Risk-based vulnerability management cannot operate in isolation within the security team. It requires collaboration with IT operations, application owners, compliance officers, and executive leadership. These stakeholders must understand the rationale behind prioritization decisions and support the allocation of resources for timely remediation. Building this shared understanding fosters a culture where risk is managed holistically, and decisions are made with both technical accuracy and strategic foresight.

One of the challenges in adopting a risk-based approach is balancing risk tolerance with operational demands. Not every vulnerability can or should be fixed immediately. In some cases, patching may introduce downtime, disrupt services, or conflict with other business requirements. Organizations must determine their acceptable level of risk and document decisions to defer remediation based on sound reasoning. This transparency is vital for accountability and for maintaining a defensible security posture in the face of regulatory scrutiny or security incidents.

Measuring the effectiveness of risk-based vulnerability management is an ongoing process. Organizations must track metrics such as time to remediate high-risk vulnerabilities, the number of critical vulnerabilities left unaddressed over time, and the alignment of remediation efforts with actual threat activity. These metrics help assess whether the risk model is functioning as intended and identify areas for improvement. Over time, this continuous feedback loop allows the model to evolve and adapt to changing business environments and threat landscapes.

Furthermore, this approach aligns security more closely with business resilience. It encourages organizations to think beyond the technical realm and consider how vulnerabilities translate into potential disruptions, financial losses, reputational damage, and regulatory consequences. By framing vulnerability management in terms of business impact, security teams gain greater support from leadership and can justify investments in tools, personnel, and processes that strengthen the organization's overall defense posture.

Risk-based vulnerability management ultimately empowers organizations to act strategically, making the best use of limited time, money, and manpower. It replaces arbitrary patching cycles with informed decision-making and shifts the focus from volume to value. In doing so, it transforms vulnerability management from a reactive chore into a proactive, business-aligned discipline that actively reduces the organization's exposure to real-world threats.

Asset Inventory and Classification

Asset inventory and classification are foundational elements of any effective vulnerability management strategy. Without a clear and accurate understanding of what assets exist within an organization's environment, where they are located, what roles they play, and how critical they are to business operations, it is impossible to assess risk or prioritize remediation effectively. Every vulnerability exists in the context of an asset, and managing those vulnerabilities begins with knowing the full scope and nature of the assets they affect.

An asset, in the context of cybersecurity, refers to any hardware, software, system, data repository, or service that holds value to the organization. This includes servers, endpoints, network devices, cloud resources, applications, databases, and even operational technology in industrial settings. Assets can be physical or virtual, on-premises or in the cloud, managed or unmanaged. The growing complexity of modern IT environments, especially with the rise of hybrid infrastructures and remote work, has made asset discovery and management more challenging than ever. Yet, this complexity makes the need for accurate asset inventory even more critical.

Establishing a comprehensive asset inventory is the first step. This process involves identifying all devices and systems connected to the organization's network, including those that may not be officially managed by IT. Shadow IT, such as personal laptops, unauthorized applications, or third-party tools, often escapes traditional oversight but can still introduce vulnerabilities into the environment. Discovery tools, network scans, endpoint agents, and integration with configuration management databases can assist in identifying and cataloging these assets. However, technology alone is not sufficient. A process must be in place to ensure the inventory remains current, with updates made as new assets are introduced and old ones decommissioned.

Once assets have been identified, the next crucial step is classification. Classification involves organizing assets according to various attributes such as type, ownership, location, function, and criticality. This is where security begins to intersect with business context. For instance, two servers might appear identical in terms of operating system and software stack, but one might host sensitive customer data while the other supports a non-critical test environment. Without proper classification, both might be treated with the same urgency during vulnerability assessments, which would be a misallocation of effort and resources.

Understanding the criticality of assets allows organizations to align vulnerability management with risk. If a vulnerability is discovered in an asset that plays a vital role in financial transactions or regulatory compliance, it should be prioritized for remediation above others, regardless of its technical severity score. This approach demands collaboration across departments to determine the business value of each asset. IT may know the configuration and dependencies of a system, but only the business units can articulate its importance to operations, customer service, or revenue generation.

Furthermore, asset classification supports the implementation of tailored security controls. Systems that are deemed critical or high-risk can be subjected to stricter monitoring, more frequent vulnerability scans, and expedited patching cycles. Less critical assets may follow standard maintenance schedules, allowing the organization to focus its limited resources where they are most needed. In this way, classification becomes a tool for strategic decision-making, not just administrative organization.

Accurate asset inventories and classifications also play a central role in incident response. When a security incident occurs, knowing exactly what systems are involved, what data they contain, and who owns them enables faster and more effective mitigation. If responders must first determine whether an affected system is a development server or a production database, valuable time is lost. An up-to-date inventory, coupled with proper classification, ensures that incident response teams can act quickly and with precision.

In the context of compliance and audits, asset inventory and classification are frequently required controls. Regulatory frameworks such as HIPAA, PCI-DSS, and ISO 27001 mandate that organizations maintain an understanding of their systems and data flows. Auditors often request evidence that inventories are maintained, reviewed, and validated on a regular basis. Organizations that neglect these practices not only expose themselves to operational risk but may also face financial penalties or reputational damage if they fall short of compliance obligations.

The dynamic nature of modern environments means that inventory and classification must be treated as continuous processes rather than one-time projects. New assets are constantly being added to the network, whether through software deployments, hardware refreshes, or mergers and acquisitions. Likewise, assets can change classification over time as their role in the business evolves. A server used for internal analytics today may be repurposed to handle customer-facing applications tomorrow. Regular review cycles, automated discovery mechanisms, and integration with change management processes are necessary to maintain accuracy and relevance.

Organizations must also consider the granularity of their classification schemes. While it may be tempting to keep classifications broad for simplicity, more detailed categorizations provide better insights for vulnerability management. Categories such as business unit, application owner, data sensitivity, uptime requirements, and external exposure all contribute to a richer understanding of risk. The more precisely assets are described, the more effectively security efforts can be focused and aligned with organizational priorities.

Ultimately, asset inventory and classification serve as the bedrock upon which all other vulnerability management activities are built. They provide the visibility and context required to interpret scan results, assess impact, and coordinate response. They connect technical vulnerabilities to the real-world systems and processes they affect, transforming abstract risks into tangible business concerns. Without this foundation, even the most advanced tools and sophisticated analytics will fall short, because the data they rely on will be incomplete or misaligned with reality. A disciplined and ongoing focus on asset inventory and classification enables organizations to build a structured, scalable, and risk-aware vulnerability management program that can adapt to change and respond to threats with clarity and confidence.

Identifying Critical Infrastructure

Identifying critical infrastructure within an organization is a vital step in establishing a strong and effective vulnerability management program. Critical infrastructure encompasses the systems, services, assets, and technologies whose failure would have a significant impact on the continuity, security, and functionality of essential business operations. The process of identifying what is truly critical requires more than technical knowledge; it demands a deep understanding of the organization's mission, business processes, regulatory obligations, and dependencies across both physical and digital domains.

In most organizations, not all infrastructure is created equal. While every asset and system may have some role to play, there is always a subset of infrastructure that is vital to business continuity, safety, or compliance. These are the systems that, if compromised, could cause major financial loss, legal exposure, reputational damage, or even endanger human lives, depending on the nature of the business. Therefore, the goal of identifying critical infrastructure is not to label everything as important, but to distinguish the systems that truly require heightened attention, protection, and prioritization in a risk-based security strategy.

The identification process begins with a mapping of business functions to the technology stack that supports them. This involves engaging with business leaders, application owners, and process managers to understand which operations are mission-critical and which systems are indispensable for those operations. These conversations often reveal dependencies that may not be immediately obvious. For instance, a billing application might be deemed critical, but its availability could depend on a background job scheduler or a database server that is not directly customer-facing. Without identifying those dependencies, a vulnerability in a supporting component might be overlooked until it leads to disruption.

It is important to recognize that critical infrastructure varies significantly across industries and organizations. In a hospital, critical systems may include electronic medical records, diagnostic imaging devices, and patient monitoring systems. In a financial institution, core banking platforms, payment processing systems, and trading networks are likely to be top priorities. For manufacturers, industrial control systems and supply chain platforms may be essential. Understanding these sector-specific requirements is key to tailoring vulnerability management to the unique risks each organization faces.

Once critical systems have been identified, they must be documented, tagged, and integrated into security monitoring and response frameworks. This step enables organizations to prioritize the protection of these assets and focus vulnerability scanning, patching, and hardening efforts where they matter most. It also enables better response coordination when incidents occur. For example, if a vulnerability is discovered in a critical database supporting the payroll system, having it flagged as critical ensures it receives appropriate attention and resources for swift remediation.

A significant challenge in identifying critical infrastructure is the dynamic nature of business and technology. Systems that are critical today may not be tomorrow, and new dependencies can emerge with the introduction of new applications, services, or business models. Cloud migration, mergers and acquisitions, and digital transformation efforts all bring changes that can shift what is considered critical. Therefore, the process of identifying critical infrastructure must be iterative and ongoing. Regular reviews, combined with input from stakeholders across the organization, are essential to ensure the classification remains accurate and aligned with the current state of operations.

Another complicating factor is the growing interconnectivity between systems. In today's digital ecosystems, critical infrastructure may depend on third-party platforms, cloud service providers, and external vendors. These dependencies extend the attack surface and introduce additional risk. Identifying critical infrastructure must, therefore, include an assessment of external connections and service providers. A disruption in a cloud provider's storage platform or a vulnerability in a vendor-supplied API can have cascading effects on internal critical systems. Organizations must understand not only what infrastructure they own and operate, but also the external elements that underpin their critical services.

Data plays a central role in determining criticality. Systems that handle sensitive personal data, financial records, intellectual property, or proprietary algorithms often rise to the level of critical infrastructure simply due to the value and risk associated with their contents. The loss, corruption, or unauthorized disclosure of such data can have consequences that extend far beyond IT concerns. Therefore, data classification should be integrated with infrastructure assessment, ensuring that systems supporting or storing critical data are appropriately prioritized in the security hierarchy.

Operational technology adds another layer of complexity to the identification process. In industries such as energy, transportation, manufacturing, and utilities, physical systems controlled by software can be just as critical as digital systems. Programmable logic controllers, sensors, and industrial control systems are often older, harder to patch, and more vulnerable to disruption. Yet they may be responsible for keeping essential services operational. Identifying these as part of the critical infrastructure inventory ensures they receive the specialized attention and controls they require, even if they do not conform to traditional IT norms.

Cultural awareness is also important in this process. Different departments and stakeholders may have divergent views on what constitutes critical infrastructure. Security teams must navigate these perspectives, mediate conflicting priorities, and arrive at a shared understanding of what systems are most vital to the organization as a whole. This may involve conducting business impact assessments, risk modeling, and tabletop exercises that simulate the consequences of system failures. These exercises often reveal surprising interdependencies and highlight assets that were previously overlooked or undervalued.

Finally, identifying critical infrastructure sets the stage for more mature security practices across the organization. It allows for differentiated treatment of assets, enabling tiered vulnerability management and tailored incident response plans. It supports the development of service level agreements for patching timelines and system recovery. It also provides a foundation for compliance efforts, audit readiness, and communication with regulators. In times of crisis, knowing which systems are critical can mean the difference between a controlled response and widespread disruption.

Identifying critical infrastructure is not merely an inventory task; it is a strategic process that binds cybersecurity efforts to business resilience. It requires cross-functional collaboration, technical insight, and a forward-looking perspective on how technology underpins core services. By investing the time and effort to define and protect critical systems, organizations can build a vulnerability management program that is both efficient and deeply aligned with their mission.

The Role of Threat Intelligence

The role of threat intelligence in vulnerability management is increasingly indispensable in a world where cyber threats evolve with alarming speed. Traditional vulnerability management approaches that rely solely on static severity ratings or internal system scans no longer provide sufficient protection against the realities of a dynamic threat landscape. Threat intelligence introduces the contextual awareness that transforms vulnerability management from a purely technical function into a strategic discipline that adapts to real-world conditions. It allows organizations to understand not only what vulnerabilities exist but which ones are most likely to be exploited, by whom, and in what manner.

Threat intelligence is the collection, analysis, and application of information about current and emerging cyber threats. This information includes data on attacker tactics, techniques, and procedures, commonly known as TTPs, as well as insights into threat actor motivations, targets, and infrastructure. It comes from a wide variety of sources, including open-source intelligence, dark web monitoring, information sharing platforms, government advisories, and commercial threat intelligence feeds. When ingested and correlated with internal vulnerability data, threat intelligence provides clarity on which vulnerabilities present the greatest risk in a given context.

In vulnerability management, one of the most valuable applications of threat intelligence is in the prioritization process. Not all vulnerabilities carry equal risk, even if they share the same technical severity score. A vulnerability with a CVSS score of 9.8 may seem like an urgent concern, but if it is not being actively exploited and is located on a system with limited exposure, its actual risk might be lower than a seemingly moderate vulnerability that is currently under attack by ransomware groups. Threat intelligence helps bridge this gap by providing real-time or near-real-time indicators that reflect the actual behavior of adversaries in the wild.

By integrating threat intelligence into vulnerability management platforms, organizations gain the ability to correlate vulnerability scan results with known exploitation data. This process, often referred to as threat-based prioritization, enables security teams to focus on vulnerabilities that are under active exploitation or are part of known threat campaigns. This greatly improves the efficiency of remediation efforts, as it allows organizations to apply their limited resources to the most pressing risks. Without this intelligence, teams risk spending valuable time patching vulnerabilities that are unlikely to be exploited while leaving themselves exposed to more immediate threats.

Moreover, threat intelligence provides insights into the behavior and capabilities of specific threat actors. Understanding which groups are targeting an organization's sector, region, or technology stack enables more focused risk assessments. For instance, if a new vulnerability in a widely used enterprise software platform is disclosed, threat intelligence can reveal whether it is being exploited by a group known to target financial institutions or healthcare providers. This information allows organizations to weigh the relevance of the threat based on their own profile and exposure. It also enables the anticipation of attack patterns and the strengthening of defenses in specific areas likely to be targeted.

Threat intelligence also plays a critical role in detecting and responding to zero-day vulnerabilities. While zero-days are, by definition, vulnerabilities that are unknown to the public or the vendor, certain indicators can suggest that a system or application may be vulnerable to emerging threats. Early signs of unusual activity, threat actor chatter on underground forums, or new exploits being tested in controlled environments can provide valuable warning signals. Organizations that monitor these indicators are better positioned to implement temporary mitigations or heightened monitoring while waiting for official patches to be released.

The usefulness of threat intelligence is not limited to technical indicators or raw data feeds. Human intelligence and analytical reporting add another layer of value. Detailed reports that examine attacker motivations, campaign timelines, and geopolitical factors can guide long-term security planning and policy development. These insights can also influence broader business decisions, such as choosing third-party vendors, investing in specific technologies, or expanding into certain markets. When security leaders have access to threat intelligence that includes strategic-level analysis, they can better align vulnerability management with organizational risk tolerance and business objectives.

For threat intelligence to have a meaningful impact, it must be actionable. Raw data without context or prioritization can overwhelm security teams and create more confusion than clarity. Therefore, threat intelligence platforms often include enrichment features that categorize vulnerabilities based on exploit maturity, availability of weaponized code, prevalence in the wild, and relevance to specific sectors. These enriched insights support faster decision-making and allow security teams to automate elements of their response, such as creating patching tickets for high-risk vulnerabilities or escalating critical findings to incident response teams.

Collaboration and information sharing further amplify the role of threat intelligence. Participating in industry-specific intelligence sharing groups or government-backed platforms enables organizations to learn from peers, detect coordinated attacks, and contribute to a broader understanding of the threat landscape. This collective intelligence improves the quality and relevance of threat data and helps build a more resilient cybersecurity community. It also enhances the organization's own threat detection capabilities by providing a wider lens through which to view emerging risks.

A mature vulnerability management program must include continuous threat intelligence integration as a core function. This requires not only tools and feeds but also skilled analysts who can interpret the data and align it with the organization's unique environment. Investing in threat intelligence is not about collecting more data, but about enabling smarter actions. As threat actors grow more sophisticated and their tactics become more adaptive, organizations must evolve their defenses accordingly. Threat intelligence ensures that vulnerability management is not simply about fixing problems after they are found, but about anticipating threats before they materialize and reducing the attack surface with strategic precision.

Vulnerability Scanning Fundamentals

Vulnerability scanning is one of the most fundamental components of a comprehensive vulnerability management program. It provides the technical visibility needed to identify security weaknesses across an organization's IT environment. These scans systematically examine systems, networks, and applications for known vulnerabilities, misconfigurations, outdated software, missing patches, and deviations from security best practices. Without routine and accurate vulnerability scanning, organizations are effectively blind to the weaknesses that adversaries could exploit. Understanding how these scans function, what their capabilities and limitations are, and how to use their results effectively is essential for reducing risk and strengthening overall security posture.

At its core, a vulnerability scan involves using specialized software tools to detect vulnerabilities by comparing the configurations and versions of operating systems, software applications, and network devices against a database of known vulnerabilities. These databases are continually updated to reflect the latest findings from security researchers, software vendors, and industry sources. The scan does not typically exploit the vulnerabilities it identifies; rather, it looks for signs that the conditions required for the vulnerability to exist are present. This approach ensures that scans are non-disruptive, allowing them to be performed in production environments with minimal risk of causing downtime.

There are two primary types of vulnerability scanning: authenticated and unauthenticated. Authenticated scans involve providing the scanner with valid credentials to access systems and gather detailed information. These scans can evaluate system configurations, installed software, registry settings, and more, resulting in higher accuracy and fewer false positives. Unauthenticated scans, on the other hand, simulate an external attack by scanning the system as an outsider without credentials. While these scans are useful for assessing perimeter defenses and identifying externally visible vulnerabilities, they generally offer less depth. A well-rounded vulnerability management program uses both types of scans to achieve comprehensive coverage.

The scanning process itself involves several stages, beginning with asset discovery. Before scanning for vulnerabilities, the tool must identify what devices are present on the network and gather basic information such as IP addresses, operating systems, open ports, and services. This discovery phase is crucial because it defines the scope of the scan and ensures that new or unmanaged assets are not overlooked. Following discovery, the scanner probes each asset using various protocols to determine the software versions, configurations, and system details needed to match them against known vulnerabilities.

Timing and frequency are important considerations in vulnerability scanning. Some organizations scan their environments weekly or monthly, while others opt for continuous scanning. The right frequency depends on the nature of the business, the criticality of the systems, compliance requirements, and the organization's risk tolerance. High-frequency scanning provides greater agility in detecting newly introduced vulnerabilities but can place additional load on systems and networks. Careful planning is needed to ensure that scans do not interfere with business operations, especially in environments with sensitive performance requirements.

Another important consideration is the scope of the scans. Organizations must define which assets are to be scanned and at what depth. Scanning all systems with equal intensity may seem thorough, but it is not always efficient or necessary. Critical systems, public-facing assets, and high-value targets should receive deeper and more frequent scrutiny, while low-risk systems might be scanned on a less aggressive schedule. This strategic targeting ensures that resources are directed where they will have the most impact and reduces the chances of being overwhelmed by low-priority findings.

One of the most common challenges in vulnerability scanning is managing the volume of results. A single scan can yield thousands of findings, many of which may be minor issues or false positives. Without context, these results can become noise, overwhelming security teams and delaying the remediation of truly critical vulnerabilities. Effective filtering, prioritization, and validation are necessary to extract actionable insights from scan reports. Integrating scan results with asset classification, business impact assessments, and threat intelligence allows organizations to sort vulnerabilities by risk rather than by severity alone.

The quality of a scan also depends heavily on the configuration of the scanning tool. Improperly configured scans can miss critical vulnerabilities or generate misleading results. Security teams must take care to tune their scanners according to the specific characteristics of their environment. This includes setting appropriate scan schedules, configuring authentication properly, ensuring up-to-date vulnerability databases, and excluding systems where scanning might cause disruption. Regular testing and validation of scanner accuracy is also important to ensure that the results remain reliable over time.

Vulnerability scanning is not a one-time activity but part of a continuous cycle. As new systems are added, software is updated, and threat actors evolve, the vulnerability landscape shifts. Regular scanning provides a snapshot of the current state of security and helps track the effectiveness of remediation efforts. Comparing scan results over time allows security teams to monitor trends, measure progress, and identify recurring issues. This historical perspective is valuable for strategic planning and for demonstrating security improvements to stakeholders and auditors.

Integration with other security tools and workflows further enhances the value of vulnerability scanning. When scan results are fed into ticketing systems, patch management platforms, security information and event management (SIEM) solutions, and risk dashboards, they become part of a broader security ecosystem. This integration supports automation, accountability, and better decision-making across departments. It ensures that findings are not only detected but also addressed and resolved in a timely manner.

Ultimately, the goal of vulnerability scanning is not just to find weaknesses but to enable the remediation of those weaknesses in alignment with the organization's goals and capabilities. When used effectively, scanning tools serve as an early warning system, a compliance aid, and a performance metric all in one. They illuminate the gaps that might otherwise remain hidden and provide the foundation upon which risk-based vulnerability management decisions are made. By mastering the fundamentals of scanning—accuracy, frequency, prioritization, and integration—organizations can build a more responsive and resilient defense posture in the face of a constantly evolving threat environment.

Configuring Scanning Tools Effectively

Configuring scanning tools effectively is essential to the success of any vulnerability management program. The utility of a vulnerability scanner does not lie solely in its ability to detect weaknesses, but in how well it is aligned with the specific environment in which it operates. Proper configuration ensures that scans are comprehensive, accurate, efficient, and relevant to the organization's risk profile. Misconfigured tools can lead to false positives, missed vulnerabilities, system disruptions, and an overwhelming volume of unprioritized data. In contrast, a well-tuned scanner delivers actionable insights that drive timely and targeted remediation.

The configuration process begins with understanding the scope and objectives of the vulnerability scanning initiative. It is crucial to determine whether the scans are intended for internal systems, external-facing assets, cloud environments, containers, or a combination of these. Each domain has different characteristics and requires specific scanning strategies. External scans, for example, simulate what an attacker sees from outside the organization's perimeter, while internal scans probe behind the firewall to uncover vulnerabilities that could be exploited by insiders or once initial access is gained. Knowing the target environment influences which scanning methods, protocols, and credentials need to be configured.

One of the most impactful aspects of scanner configuration is the use of authentication. Authenticated scans allow the scanning tool to log into systems and perform a deeper and more accurate analysis. They can access configuration files, system settings, installed patches, and user permissions that are not visible during unauthenticated scans. Configuring the appropriate credentials for each target platform—whether Windows, Linux, database, or application—is critical for maximizing scan coverage. Credentials must be tested and validated in advance to ensure that they grant the necessary read-only access without violating organizational policies or causing unintentional changes to systems.

Another important element is tuning the scanning profiles. Most scanning tools come with predefined templates or policies that cover common use cases, but these often require customization to suit the organization's unique needs. Configuring which types of vulnerabilities to look for, which ports to scan, what services to interrogate, and how deeply to probe can significantly affect the accuracy and efficiency of the scan. In some cases, overly aggressive scans can overwhelm network devices or cause instability in sensitive systems. Therefore, it is essential to balance thoroughness with stability by tailoring scan intensity settings and excluding systems that are not scan-tolerant or that require special handling.

Scheduling scans is also a critical aspect of effective configuration. Organizations must determine how frequently different assets should be scanned, and at what times, to minimize operational disruption. High-availability systems or performance-sensitive environments may need to be scanned during off-peak hours. On the other hand, critical systems might require more frequent assessments to ensure rapid detection of newly introduced vulnerabilities. Scanning schedules should be coordinated with maintenance windows, patch cycles, and change management processes to avoid conflicts and ensure that the results reflect the current state of the infrastructure.

Network segmentation and access control present additional configuration challenges. In environments with multiple subnets, virtual private clouds, or air-gapped segments, the scanning tool must be able to reach all intended targets. This may require deploying scan engines in different network zones or configuring firewall rules to allow scanning traffic. Failure to account for network topology can result in incomplete coverage and a false sense of security. Regular connectivity testing and validation should be incorporated into the configuration process to ensure that all systems within scope are reachable and responsive.

Exclusion rules are another important configuration feature that help refine the scan scope and prevent unwanted disruptions. Some systems, such as legacy servers, industrial control devices, or applications with known sensitivities, may not handle active scanning well. Others may be maintained by third-party vendors or governed by contractual restrictions. In such cases, these assets should be excluded from routine scans and handled using alternative assessment methods. Documenting these exclusions and reviewing them periodically ensures transparency and accountability while maintaining the integrity of the scanning process.

The configuration of alerting and reporting mechanisms should also not be overlooked. Scanning tools can generate vast amounts of data, but that data must be delivered in a format that is understandable, actionable, and tailored to the needs of different stakeholders. Configuring custom dashboards, automated reports, and integration with ticketing systems or security information and event management platforms helps streamline workflows and ensures that the right people are notified when high-risk vulnerabilities are detected. Reports should be categorized by risk level, asset criticality, and remediation status to enable efficient tracking and response.

Maintaining an up-to-date vulnerability database is an ongoing aspect of scanner configuration. Most scanning tools rely on periodic updates to their signature libraries in order to detect the latest vulnerabilities. Ensuring that these updates are applied regularly and without delay is vital for maintaining scanning accuracy. In some cases, custom vulnerability checks may need to be developed and configured for proprietary systems or emerging threats that are not yet covered by the standard database.

Effective configuration also includes enabling logging and audit capabilities. Detailed logs of scanning activity, results, and system interactions provide a forensic trail that can be valuable during incident investigations or compliance audits. Configuring logging to capture meaningful information without overwhelming storage capacity requires careful planning, but the benefits in terms of visibility and accountability are significant.

Training and documentation are essential final elements in the configuration process. Security teams must be trained on how to properly configure, run, interpret, and troubleshoot scanning tools. Documentation of all configuration settings, scanning schedules, exclusion lists, credentials used, and change history ensures continuity and knowledge retention. This is especially important in environments with high staff turnover or shared operational responsibilities.

Ultimately, configuring scanning tools effectively is a combination of technical precision, environmental awareness, and strategic alignment with organizational goals. It transforms vulnerability scanning from a basic operational task into a powerful risk management function. With the right configuration, scanning tools can deliver high-fidelity results that support timely remediation, informed decision-making, and continuous improvement across the entire security program. The effort invested in configuration upfront yields substantial returns in terms of accuracy, efficiency, and impact, enabling security teams to operate with confidence in an ever-changing threat landscape.

Interpreting Scan Results

Interpreting scan results is one of the most critical and often underestimated aspects of vulnerability management. While running a scan may seem like a technical operation, understanding what the results actually mean and how they should be acted upon requires a blend of technical knowledge, contextual awareness, and risk-based thinking. The output of a vulnerability scan typically includes a list of detected vulnerabilities, affected assets, severity ratings, and suggested remediation actions. However, without careful interpretation, this data can be misleading, overwhelming, or even counterproductive. The raw output must be translated into meaningful insights that support timely and informed decision-making.

At first glance, scan results often appear as an extensive list of issues, each accompanied by a severity score, usually based on the Common Vulnerability Scoring System. While CVSS scores provide a useful baseline for assessing the technical severity of a vulnerability, they are not sufficient by themselves to determine actual risk. A critical vulnerability on a development server with no internet access is not the same as the same vulnerability on a public-facing application handling sensitive data. The context in which a vulnerability exists dramatically influences its significance, which means that security teams must look beyond the score to understand the broader picture.

Interpreting scan results begins with establishing asset context. This means understanding the role of the affected asset within the organization, its exposure level, and its importance to business operations. When a vulnerability is detected, the first question should not be how severe it is technically, but how critical the asset is and how easily the vulnerability could be exploited in that specific environment. This requires cross-referencing scan results with asset inventory data, classifications, and threat intelligence. For example, a medium-severity vulnerability on a server that is frequently targeted by attackers may demand more urgent attention than a high-severity flaw in a low-risk system.

False positives are another common issue that complicates the interpretation of scan results. These occur when the scanner flags a vulnerability that is either not actually present or not exploitable due to compensating controls. For instance, a scanner might detect that a system is running a version of software known to be vulnerable, but in practice, the vulnerable component may be disabled or protected by additional layers of security. These inaccuracies can lead to wasted time and resources if not properly vetted. Security teams must verify findings before initiating remediation, particularly for high-impact vulnerabilities, by manually checking configurations or using supplemental tools for validation.

Equally challenging are false negatives, where the scanner fails to detect an existing vulnerability. These can occur due to network segmentation, access restrictions, or misconfigured scan settings. Interpreting scan results must also involve understanding what is missing. If an area of the network is not covered or if certain systems consistently return incomplete results, this should raise red flags. Scan logs and coverage reports should be reviewed regularly to ensure that the scanner is functioning as expected and that no significant blind spots are being overlooked.

Once validated, the next step is prioritization. This process transforms raw scan data into a manageable and actionable set of tasks. Prioritization must be guided by a combination of factors including severity, exploitability, business impact, asset criticality, and current threat activity. Integrating real-time threat intelligence can help determine if a particular vulnerability is being actively exploited in the wild, which should elevate its priority. Similarly, if a vulnerability affects a regulatory asset or a system that handles sensitive information, it should receive immediate attention regardless of its technical rating. This approach helps avoid the common pitfall of treating all findings equally, which often leads to delayed remediation of truly dangerous vulnerabilities.

Reporting is another essential part of interpreting scan results. Different stakeholders require different levels of detail. Technical teams need in-depth information about affected files, patch availability, and configuration settings. In contrast, executives and business leaders need high-level summaries that highlight trends, risks, and progress toward remediation goals. Configuring scanning tools to generate tailored reports ensures that the right people receive the right information. Reports should also provide historical comparisons to track progress, such as the number of high-risk vulnerabilities over time or the average time to remediation. These metrics support continuous improvement and demonstrate the effectiveness of the vulnerability management program.

Understanding scan results also means recognizing patterns. Repeated vulnerabilities in the same systems may indicate deeper issues with configuration management, patching processes, or change control. Identifying trends helps uncover systemic problems that cannot be solved by fixing individual vulnerabilities alone. For example, if multiple servers repeatedly report outdated software versions, it may suggest gaps in the patch deployment pipeline. Interpreting scan data at this higher level enables organizations to move beyond reactive responses and start addressing root causes.

In complex environments, correlating scan results with other data sources adds additional value. When scan findings are integrated with endpoint detection and response systems, security incident and event management platforms, or configuration management databases, they become part of a broader security intelligence picture. This correlation helps validate findings, enrich them with context, and align them with ongoing investigations or incidents. For instance, if a vulnerability is detected on a system that has also triggered suspicious activity alerts, this convergence of evidence can inform more urgent and targeted action.

Ultimately, the goal of interpreting scan results is to reduce risk by enabling informed decision-making. This requires a disciplined process that starts with validating the accuracy of the data, continues with contextual prioritization, and ends with clear communication and action. Every scan is a snapshot of the organization's current security state, but without careful interpretation, it is just a collection of numbers and technical jargon. Turning that data into knowledge—and knowledge into action—is where the true value of vulnerability scanning lies. When done effectively, the interpretation process ensures that security efforts are focused, resources are used wisely, and vulnerabilities are addressed in a way that aligns with both operational needs and strategic goals.

Managing False Positives and Negatives

Managing false positives and false negatives is a persistent and critical challenge in any vulnerability management program. These issues, if not addressed properly, can severely undermine the efficiency, accuracy, and credibility of security operations. False positives occur when a vulnerability scanner incorrectly reports the existence of a vulnerability that is not actually present or exploitable, while false negatives represent the opposite scenario, where a genuine vulnerability goes undetected. Both types of errors can lead to misinformed decision-making, misallocation of resources, and potentially dangerous blind spots in an organization's security posture.

False positives can be particularly disruptive because they consume valuable time and effort from security and IT teams. When a vulnerability is reported, it typically triggers a process that includes validation, risk assessment, and remediation planning. If the reported issue turns out to be a false positive, all of that work has been wasted. Over time, repeated false positives can erode trust in the scanning tools and create a sense of fatigue among team members. In some organizations, this leads to critical alerts being dismissed or overlooked, simply because so many have turned out to be inaccurate. This creates a dangerous situation where real threats may be missed due to overexposure to erroneous data.

The root causes of false positives are varied. Sometimes they are the result of outdated or overly aggressive vulnerability signatures that match benign system behavior. In other cases, they stem from misconfigured scanning tools that incorrectly interpret system information or lack the necessary permissions to perform accurate checks. For example, if a scanner is not provided with administrative credentials, it may fail to verify that a patch has been applied and wrongly assume the system is vulnerable. Additionally, software version detection can be imprecise if versioning conventions vary or if custom configurations obscure standard markers.

Effectively managing false positives begins with validation. This involves verifying scan results manually or with supplemental tools before initiating remediation. Security teams must cross-check the details of each finding with actual system configurations, patch levels, and operational data. Where possible, validation should be automated using scripts or integrated tools that can interrogate systems directly and confirm whether a vulnerability truly exists. In complex environments, creating validation playbooks or standard operating procedures helps ensure consistency and reduce the time required to confirm findings.

Communication between security and IT operations teams is essential in this process. Security teams may identify potential vulnerabilities, but operations teams have direct access to the systems in question and can provide context or evidence that either supports or refutes the findings. Collaboration reduces finger-pointing, accelerates validation, and helps maintain a unified front in addressing risk. Involving application owners and system administrators in the validation process also builds a shared understanding of the environment, which can lead to fewer misinterpretations and more accurate scan configurations over time.

False negatives are equally concerning, though often more insidious. Because they represent vulnerabilities that have not been detected, they create a false sense of security. Systems may be assumed to be safe when in fact they are exposed to exploitation. False negatives can occur for a number of reasons. Limited scan coverage is a common culprit. If certain systems or network segments are not included in the scan scope, vulnerabilities in those areas will never be detected. Similarly, insufficient permissions, network segmentation, or endpoint security controls can block scanners from collecting the information they need to identify vulnerabilities accurately.

Another cause of false negatives lies in the limitations of the vulnerability database itself. If a new vulnerability has not yet been added to the scanning tool's signature database, it will go undetected. This highlights the importance of keeping scanning tools updated and supplementing them with real-time threat intelligence feeds. Relying solely on scheduled updates can leave an organization exposed to emerging threats. Organizations must adopt a layered approach to detection, combining traditional scanning with behavioral analysis, intrusion detection systems, and other technologies that may identify vulnerabilities based on anomalous activity rather than static indicators.

To manage false negatives effectively, organizations must conduct regular gap analyses. This includes reviewing scan coverage reports, validating that all critical systems are being scanned, and confirming that scans are completing successfully without errors. It also involves assessing whether scanning frequency is adequate to detect vulnerabilities in a timely manner. Systems that are updated frequently or exposed to the internet may require more frequent scanning to catch new issues quickly. Periodic penetration testing can serve as a check on the scanning process by attempting to discover vulnerabilities through manual techniques and comparing the results with what automated tools have reported.

Training plays an important role in reducing both false positives and negatives. Security professionals must understand how scanning tools work, what their limitations are, and how to interpret their outputs effectively. Overreliance on automation without a clear understanding of the underlying mechanics can lead to critical oversights. Teams should be trained to investigate discrepancies, ask the right questions, and know when to escalate findings for deeper analysis. Building this capability not only improves accuracy but also fosters a culture of analytical thinking and continuous improvement.

Another strategy is to tune and customize scanning tools to better fit the specific environment. Default settings are designed to be broadly applicable, but they rarely offer optimal accuracy in a unique infrastructure. Customizing scan profiles, excluding non-relevant checks, and fine-tuning thresholds can significantly reduce false positives. Conversely, ensuring that custom scripts and plugins are kept up to date and aligned with the organization's technology stack helps prevent false negatives. Configuration should be revisited regularly as the environment evolves and as lessons are learned from past scanning cycles.

Documentation and feedback loops further enhance the management of scanning inaccuracies. Each false positive or negative should be recorded, analyzed, and used to improve future scans. Lessons learned should be incorporated into tool configurations, scan policies, and team procedures. By building a feedback mechanism that captures and acts upon validation outcomes, organizations can continually refine their vulnerability management processes.

Managing false positives and negatives is not a one-time effort but an ongoing discipline that requires vigilance, collaboration, and adaptability. It is about making vulnerability management not only more efficient but more accurate, so that security teams can trust the data they rely on to make critical decisions. As environments grow more complex and threats more sophisticated, the ability to filter signal from noise will become one of the defining capabilities of successful security programs. Addressing these challenges head-on ensures that vulnerability management remains focused, credible, and aligned with the true risk landscape facing the organization.

Patch Management Strategies

Patch management strategies are at the heart of a mature vulnerability management program. Without effective patching, vulnerabilities remain open doors that attackers can exploit, regardless of how well those vulnerabilities are identified or prioritized. Patching may seem like a straightforward process—identify the fix and apply it—but in practice, it is a complex balancing act involving timing, risk assessment, operational stability, system compatibility, and coordination across multiple teams. A well-crafted patch management strategy ensures that security and functionality evolve together, minimizing risk while maintaining business continuity.

Patches are updates released by software vendors to fix bugs, enhance performance, or, most importantly from a security standpoint, address known vulnerabilities. When a vulnerability is publicly disclosed, particularly one that affects widely used systems or applications, it becomes a race against time. Threat actors rapidly create and share exploit code, and organizations must move just as quickly to apply patches and close the gap. However, in enterprise environments, rapid patching is not always feasible. Systems often have complex dependencies, custom configurations, or service-level agreements that make immediate changes difficult. This tension between urgency and stability is what makes patch management both critical and challenging.

One of the first elements of an effective patch management strategy is visibility. Organizations need a complete and accurate inventory of all hardware and software assets, including version details and patch levels. Without this visibility, it is impossible to know what systems are vulnerable or what patches need to be applied. Asset inventory tools, configuration management databases, and vulnerability scanning platforms can help track this information, but maintaining its accuracy requires ongoing effort. As systems are added, updated, or decommissioned, the inventory must be updated accordingly to ensure patching decisions are based on current data.

Once visibility is established, organizations must implement a classification system that ranks assets by criticality. This classification guides patching priorities. Systems that handle sensitive data, support critical business functions, or are exposed to the internet should be patched before lower-risk systems. Risk-based prioritization ensures that limited resources are directed where they will have the most impact. Patching every system with the same urgency is neither practical nor necessary. By focusing on high-value targets, organizations can significantly reduce risk while minimizing disruption.

Another key component is testing. Before a patch is applied to production systems, it should be thoroughly tested in a staging or development environment that mirrors the live configuration as closely as possible. Patches can introduce new bugs, cause compatibility issues, or disrupt services. Rigorous testing helps identify potential problems in advance, allowing teams to adjust configurations, coordinate downtime, or even defer a patch when necessary. However, excessive caution can lead to dangerous delays. The challenge is to test efficiently and with a clear understanding of risk tolerance. In some cases, the threat posed by an unpatched vulnerability may outweigh the risk of potential side effects.

Automation plays an increasingly important role in patch management. Automated patch deployment tools can schedule, test, and apply patches across a wide range of systems with minimal human intervention. These tools reduce the time between patch release and implementation, improve consistency, and free up staff for higher-level analysis and decision-making. However, automation must be used judiciously. Not all patches are created equal, and some systems may require manual oversight due to their complexity or business impact. A hybrid approach that combines automated patching for low-risk systems with manual review for critical assets provides the best balance between speed and control.

Communication and coordination across teams are essential to a smooth patch management process. Security teams may identify the need for a patch, but IT operations, development, and business units are often responsible for implementation. These groups must work together to schedule updates, allocate resources, and resolve issues. A lack of communication can result in missed patches, service interruptions, or duplicate efforts. Regular meetings, shared documentation, and a centralized change management system help keep everyone aligned. Clearly defined roles and responsibilities prevent confusion and ensure accountability.

Documentation and tracking are also vital. Every patching activity should be recorded, including the systems affected, the date of application, any issues encountered, and verification of successful implementation. This documentation supports audits, compliance reporting, and forensic investigations in the event of a security incident. It also provides historical data that can be used to improve future patch cycles. Patterns in patch failures, delays, or incompatibilities can highlight weaknesses in the process and guide targeted improvements.

Timing is a strategic factor in patch management. Many organizations adopt scheduled patch cycles—weekly, monthly, or quarterly—to maintain order and predictability. Scheduled cycles reduce the risk of ad hoc changes and allow time for testing and communication. However, this approach must be flexible enough to accommodate emergency patches for high-risk vulnerabilities. When critical exploits are discovered, organizations need a rapid response capability that can bypass the standard schedule and deploy fixes immediately. This requires clear criteria for determining what constitutes an emergency and predefined workflows for fast-track implementation.

In some cases, patching is not immediately possible. Legacy systems, custom applications, or operational constraints may prevent updates from being applied. In such situations, compensating controls must be implemented to mitigate the risk. These may include network segmentation, firewall rules, intrusion detection systems, or even temporary isolation of the affected system. The goal is to reduce the attack surface and prevent exploitation while working on a long-term solution. However, these controls should never become a permanent substitute for proper patching.

Patch management is not a standalone activity but part of a larger ecosystem of IT and security governance. It intersects with vulnerability management, incident response, change control, compliance, and risk management. To be effective, patching must be embedded in these broader processes, supported by policies, enforced by tools, and guided by metrics. Key performance indicators such as mean time to patch, patch success rate, and coverage of critical systems provide insight into the health of the patch management program and identify areas for improvement.

A strong patch management strategy protects the organization from known threats while maintaining the stability and performance of its systems. It requires visibility, prioritization, testing, automation, coordination, and continuous refinement. When all these elements work together, patching becomes not just a technical task but a strategic function that strengthens resilience and reduces exposure in a constantly changing threat environment.

Coordinating with IT Operations

Coordinating with IT operations is a fundamental requirement for the success of any vulnerability management program. While security teams are typically responsible for identifying vulnerabilities and determining which ones need to be addressed, it is IT operations that usually bears the responsibility for implementing the fixes. This division of responsibilities can create friction if not managed properly. Effective coordination bridges the gap between detection and remediation, transforming what could be a source of conflict into a productive collaboration that strengthens the organization's overall security posture.

The relationship between cybersecurity and IT operations is often complex. Security teams tend to operate with a risk-reduction mindset, driven by the need to address threats quickly and thoroughly. Their focus is on identifying gaps and mitigating risks as soon as possible. In contrast, IT operations is primarily concerned with system stability, performance, and uptime. Their mandate is to ensure the continuous availability of services, often under tight resource constraints and performance expectations. As a result, their approach to implementing changes, including patches or configuration adjustments, is usually more cautious and deliberate. This difference in priorities can create tension if not acknowledged and addressed through structured coordination.

One of the most important aspects of coordination is clear communication. Security teams must not only report vulnerabilities but also provide detailed context that helps IT operations understand the nature of the issue, the potential impact, and the recommended course of action. Simply handing over a long list of vulnerabilities with severity scores is not enough. Effective communication includes explanations of why certain vulnerabilities are prioritized, what systems are affected, how the vulnerabilities could be exploited, and what remediation steps are necessary. When this information is presented in a business-aligned context, it makes it easier for IT operations to evaluate, plan, and act.

Establishing shared goals is another critical step in fostering collaboration. Both security and IT operations ultimately want the same thing: a resilient, stable, and secure environment. By aligning vulnerability management efforts with broader business objectives— such as maintaining uptime, meeting compliance standards, and protecting customer data—security and operations teams can work toward a common purpose. This shared vision allows for compromises and trade-offs when necessary. For example, if a critical patch must be applied urgently but may cause downtime, both teams can coordinate to schedule the update during a maintenance window, ensuring that risk is reduced without disrupting operations.

Coordination must also be supported by formal processes. Change management frameworks provide a structured way to evaluate, approve, and implement changes across systems. Vulnerability remediation actions, particularly those involving patches or configuration changes, should be integrated into these processes. This ensures that all stakeholders are informed, risks are assessed, dependencies are understood, and implementation is planned in a controlled manner. It also provides an audit trail for accountability and compliance. When vulnerability management is tightly integrated with change management, it reduces surprises, increases transparency, and improves the consistency of remediation efforts.

Regular meetings between security and IT operations are essential for maintaining alignment. These meetings should focus on reviewing recent scan results, discussing remediation priorities, planning upcoming changes, and addressing any challenges or bottlenecks. Establishing a cadence for these discussions—whether weekly, biweekly, or monthly—creates a rhythm that keeps both teams synchronized. Over time, these interactions build trust, reduce miscommunication, and create a sense of shared responsibility for security outcomes.

Another key element of coordination is the use of shared tools and data sources. When security and operations teams rely on separate systems with different views of the environment, confusion and delays are inevitable. Integrating vulnerability management platforms with IT service management tools, configuration management databases, and asset inventory systems provides a unified view that supports more efficient decision-making. For instance, when a vulnerability is identified on a server, having immediate access to ownership information, system dependencies, and change history helps IT operations plan the remediation more effectively.

Prioritization frameworks also play a role in streamlining collaboration. Not every vulnerability can be fixed immediately, and not every system requires the same level of protection. Establishing risk-based prioritization criteria—based on asset criticality, exploitability, and threat intelligence—ensures that both security and operations teams are working from the same playbook. This reduces disagreements about what should be addressed first and allows for more strategic allocation of resources.

Metrics and reporting are valuable tools for reinforcing coordination. Tracking metrics such as time to remediation, percentage of critical vulnerabilities patched, and compliance with service-level agreements helps both teams measure their performance and identify areas for improvement. When these metrics are shared across teams and discussed openly, they become a driver for accountability and continuous improvement. They also provide leadership with visibility into how effectively vulnerability management is being executed and where additional support may be needed.

Training and cross-functional education further enhance collaboration. When IT operations staff have a basic understanding of security principles and the threat landscape, they are more likely to appreciate the urgency of certain remediation tasks. Likewise, when security teams understand the operational challenges involved in deploying patches and managing infrastructure, they can set more realistic expectations and timelines. Cross-training sessions, joint tabletop exercises, and security awareness briefings all contribute to building a culture of mutual respect and cooperation.

Emergencies and zero-day vulnerabilities present unique coordination challenges. In such situations, the normal patch cycle and change management processes may not provide the speed required to respond effectively. Having predefined escalation procedures and incident response protocols ensures that both security and IT operations can act quickly and decisively. These protocols should specify who needs to be notified, how decisions will be made, and what actions should be taken. Practicing these scenarios in advance through simulation exercises helps teams prepare for high-pressure situations and avoid confusion when time is of the essence.

Ultimately, coordinating with IT operations is not a tactical concern but a strategic one. Vulnerability management cannot succeed in isolation. It requires the engagement, support, and active participation of the teams responsible for maintaining and operating the systems that support the business. By building strong partnerships based on communication, shared goals, formal processes, and mutual understanding, organizations can ensure that vulnerabilities are addressed effectively and that security becomes an integrated part of the operational fabric. This alignment turns vulnerability management into a collaborative process that enhances resilience, supports innovation, and safeguards the continuity and integrity of critical services.

The Importance of Timely Remediation

Timely remediation is one of the most critical components of a successful vulnerability management program. Discovering vulnerabilities through scanning, threat intelligence, and assessments is only the first step. The real value lies in how quickly and effectively those vulnerabilities are addressed before they can be exploited. Every day that a known vulnerability remains unpatched or unmitigated increases the risk of compromise, especially when threat actors are aware of the weakness and are actively seeking to exploit it. The time between vulnerability disclosure and exploitation is shrinking, making speed a defining factor in an organization's defensive capability.

Cybersecurity is fundamentally a race against time. When a vulnerability is publicly disclosed, particularly one with high severity or easy exploitability, it often becomes a target for attackers within hours or even minutes. Automated bots and scanners crawl the internet looking for systems that are vulnerable to known exploits, and attackers routinely leverage vulnerability feeds to prioritize targets. In many cases, proof-of-concept code is published within days of a vulnerability's announcement, and these tools quickly find their way into the hands of both opportunistic and well-resourced adversaries. This immediacy creates a window of exposure that organizations must aim to minimize through timely action.

Timely remediation reduces this window of opportunity. By rapidly addressing vulnerabilities, organizations limit the amount of time attackers have to exploit them. This is particularly important for systems that are publicly accessible, such as web applications, VPN gateways, and exposed databases. These assets are under constant scrutiny from external threats and are often targeted first in automated attacks. Rapid remediation of critical vulnerabilities in these areas is essential for maintaining a strong perimeter defense and preventing initial compromise. Internal systems, although less exposed, are also important to address in a timely manner, especially in cases where attackers have already gained a foothold within the network.

Beyond the immediate technical risk, there are operational and business implications tied to the speed of remediation. Regulatory compliance requirements often include strict guidelines on how quickly vulnerabilities must be addressed once discovered. Standards like PCI DSS, HIPAA, and NIST include timelines for patching based on severity, and failure to meet these expectations can result in penalties, legal liabilities, and reputational damage. Moreover, during audits or incident investigations, documentation of remediation timelines is often scrutinized to assess whether the organization acted responsibly. Demonstrating the ability to remediate vulnerabilities promptly shows not only operational maturity but also due diligence in protecting sensitive information.

One of the key challenges in achieving timely remediation is resource allocation. Organizations often struggle with limited staffing, competing priorities, and the operational risks associated with making changes to production environments. Applying patches or configuration changes can introduce unexpected problems, impact service availability, or require coordination across multiple departments. These complexities often lead to delays, especially when change management processes are overly rigid or lack the flexibility to respond to urgent security needs. Balancing the need for thorough testing and controlled deployment with the urgency of mitigating known risks is a difficult but necessary aspect of vulnerability management.

To support timely remediation, organizations must establish clear policies and service-level agreements that define acceptable timeframes for addressing vulnerabilities of various severities. For example, critical vulnerabilities might require remediation within 48 hours, high severity within a week, and medium within a month. These timeframes should be realistic based on the organization's capabilities, but also aggressive enough to reduce risk. Tracking compliance with these timelines helps security teams measure performance and identify systemic delays. When remediation falls outside acceptable windows, root cause analysis should be conducted to determine whether the issue was a lack of awareness, insufficient resources, procedural inefficiencies, or technical barriers.

Automation is an important enabler of speed. Automated patch management, configuration enforcement, and vulnerability scanning tools can accelerate the detection-to-remediation cycle significantly. When vulnerabilities are discovered, automated workflows can initiate patch deployment, create tickets in service management platforms, and notify responsible teams immediately. Automation reduces the dependency on manual effort, minimizes delays due to human error or oversight, and ensures a consistent response. However, automation must be carefully designed to avoid unintended consequences, particularly in environments with complex dependencies or legacy systems that may not respond well to changes.

Another critical element of timely remediation is visibility. Security and IT teams must have access to accurate, up-to-date information about which assets are affected by which vulnerabilities. Asset inventories, configuration management databases, and vulnerability management platforms must be synchronized to provide a real-time picture of risk across the environment. Without this visibility, teams can waste valuable time investigating irrelevant systems, duplicating effort, or missing critical assets altogether. Streamlined workflows and integrated data sources enhance situational awareness and improve response times.

Leadership support is also vital. Timely remediation requires organizational commitment, not just technical capability. Security must be recognized as a business priority, and leadership must empower teams with the authority and resources to act swiftly when vulnerabilities are identified. This may mean investing in automation, allocating dedicated patching windows, or providing cross-functional training to reduce handoff delays. When leaders champion the importance of rapid remediation and make it a part of the company's culture, teams are more likely to treat it with the urgency it deserves.

Timely remediation is not just about reacting quickly but about being prepared to act when needed. This involves establishing robust processes, rehearsing emergency scenarios, and learning from past delays. Organizations that consistently meet remediation timelines do so because they have planned for it, institutionalized it, and integrated it into their daily operations. They do not scramble each time a new vulnerability is announced; instead, they execute a well-defined process that ensures a fast and effective response.

The value of timely remediation lies in its ability to prevent breaches, protect assets, and uphold trust. In the fast-paced world of cybersecurity, where threats evolve rapidly and attack surfaces are constantly shifting, the speed at which an organization can respond to known vulnerabilities can determine the difference between a secure system and a compromised one. Timely action translates into reduced exposure, enhanced resilience, and greater confidence in the organization's ability to manage and mitigate risk. It is a standard by which the effectiveness of a vulnerability management program is measured and a capability that every organization must strive to develop and sustain.

Vulnerability Prioritization Techniques

Vulnerability prioritization techniques are essential to managing the overwhelming volume of vulnerabilities that organizations face in modern IT environments. Thousands of new vulnerabilities are disclosed each year, and automated scanning tools often generate extensive lists of findings for every assessment. Remediating every vulnerability immediately is not only impractical but also unnecessary. Security teams must make informed decisions about which vulnerabilities to address first, based on a variety of technical and contextual factors. Prioritization allows organizations to allocate resources effectively, mitigate the most significant risks promptly, and avoid wasting time on vulnerabilities that pose minimal threat in their specific environment.

One of the most widely used starting points for prioritization is the Common Vulnerability Scoring System, which provides a numerical severity score from zero to ten. CVSS evaluates factors such as the ease of exploitation, the impact on confidentiality, integrity, and availability, and whether user interaction is required for exploitation. These scores help categorize vulnerabilities as low, medium, high, or critical severity. However, CVSS on its own has limitations. It provides a generic view of technical severity without considering the specific context of the affected organization. Two vulnerabilities with identical CVSS scores can represent very different levels of risk depending on asset value, network exposure, and the presence of compensating controls.

To overcome the limitations of static scoring, organizations increasingly turn to risk-based prioritization. This approach incorporates asset context, threat intelligence, and exploitability data to determine which vulnerabilities present the most urgent and realistic threats. For example, a vulnerability on a server that handles sensitive customer data and is exposed to the internet would typically be prioritized over the same vulnerability on an internal server with no critical information. Asset criticality becomes a core factor in prioritization, requiring an up-to-date asset inventory that includes information about the system's role, owner, location, and business importance.

Threat intelligence adds another layer of precision to vulnerability prioritization. If a vulnerability is known to be actively exploited by cybercriminals or nation-state actors, or if proof-of-concept exploit code has been published, the urgency of remediation increases significantly. Threat intelligence feeds and vendor advisories help organizations identify which vulnerabilities are being targeted in the wild, enabling them to adjust priorities dynamically. Some vulnerability management platforms integrate this data directly, flagging actively exploited vulnerabilities and assigning higher priority scores based on real-time threat activity.

Another technique involves evaluating exploitability. Not all vulnerabilities, even critical ones, are easily exploitable. Some require complex conditions, elevated privileges, or specific configurations that may not exist in the target environment. Prioritization frameworks often factor in whether an exploit is publicly available, how mature the exploit is, and whether it has been weaponized in malware or ransomware campaigns. Vulnerabilities with working exploits that can be deployed quickly and with minimal effort typically warrant immediate attention. Understanding exploitability helps focus efforts on issues that attackers are most likely to use.

Business impact is also a central component in prioritizing vulnerabilities. Organizations must assess the potential consequences of exploitation, not just in technical terms but also in relation to business operations, compliance obligations, and reputational harm. A vulnerability in a system that supports core financial processes or regulatory reporting may carry higher consequences than one in a test environment or a legacy application that is no longer in use. This requires close collaboration between security, IT, and business stakeholders to map vulnerabilities to business functions and understand the downstream effects of potential exploitation.

Attack surface exposure further influences prioritization. Systems directly accessible from the internet, such as public-facing web servers, email gateways, or remote access tools, are more vulnerable to external attack and should be scanned and patched more aggressively. Conversely, internal systems protected by firewalls, segmentation, or other controls may be less urgent. However, exposure is not static. Changes in network architecture, cloud deployments, and third-party integrations can alter the exposure profile of systems, requiring continuous monitoring and reevaluation of priorities.

Time-based factors also play a role. The time since vulnerability disclosure can influence attacker interest. New vulnerabilities tend to receive significant attention in the early days after disclosure, especially if they affect widely used platforms. Vulnerabilities with media coverage or association with named threats often attract attackers quickly. Additionally, vulnerabilities that remain unpatched for long periods may be viewed as low-hanging fruit by threat actors. Some prioritization models include aging as a variable, increasing the priority of unresolved issues as they linger beyond acceptable remediation windows.

Machine learning and automation are increasingly used to enhance prioritization techniques. Advanced platforms can analyze historical data, correlate vulnerability characteristics with past incidents, and predict which vulnerabilities are most likely to be exploited. These systems learn over time, refining their models based on real-world outcomes and providing recommendations that go beyond traditional scoring. By continuously analyzing data from scans, threat intelligence, and system logs, these tools can prioritize vulnerabilities with greater speed and accuracy than manual methods alone.

Another valuable prioritization technique is leveraging vulnerability grouping and correlation. Instead of evaluating vulnerabilities in isolation, teams can group related findings, such as all vulnerabilities affecting a particular application, system cluster, or business function. This approach allows for bulk remediation and reduces the overhead of handling each finding individually. Correlating vulnerabilities that share a common root cause, such as misconfigured permissions or unpatched libraries, also helps address broader security issues more efficiently. Rather than treating symptoms, this method enables teams to fix the underlying problem and prevent recurrence.

User-defined criteria are also useful for customizing prioritization based on the organization's specific environment and policies. Security teams may assign higher priority to vulnerabilities that affect systems with compliance requirements, support customer-facing applications, or fall within key performance indicators. Custom tags, labels, and filters in vulnerability management tools allow for flexible prioritization that aligns with internal goals and risk appetite.

Prioritization is not a one-time activity but an ongoing process that evolves with changes in technology, threat landscape, and business operations. Regular reviews of prioritization criteria, validation of assumptions, and adjustment of risk models are necessary to ensure relevance and effectiveness. By combining multiple techniques—technical scoring, asset criticality, threat intelligence, exploitability, business impact, and machine learning—organizations can create a prioritization strategy that is both comprehensive and adaptable.

The effectiveness of vulnerability management ultimately depends on the ability to focus on what matters most. Prioritization ensures that limited time, personnel, and budget are used wisely, that high-risk vulnerabilities are addressed before they can be exploited, and that security efforts are aligned with real-world threats and business objectives. It turns raw data into meaningful action and transforms vulnerability management from a reactive process into a proactive defense strategy.

Common Vulnerability Scoring System (CVSS)

The Common Vulnerability Scoring System, or CVSS, plays a foundational role in the field of vulnerability management. It provides a standardized framework for assessing the severity of vulnerabilities in a consistent and vendor-neutral way. The system has become the most widely adopted method for assigning numerical scores to vulnerabilities, offering organizations a structured way to prioritize security issues based on quantifiable metrics. Understanding how CVSS works, what its components are, and what its limitations might be is essential for using it effectively within a broader risk management context.

CVSS was developed by the Forum of Incident Response and Security Teams (FIRST) to enable a consistent and repeatable way to rate the severity of vulnerabilities across different software products and platforms. It helps security professionals, system administrators, and other stakeholders understand how serious a vulnerability is in terms of its potential impact on the confidentiality, integrity, and availability of systems and data. This scoring system offers a numerical scale from 0.0 to 10.0, which is further categorized into qualitative levels such as low, medium, high, and critical severity. These scores help prioritize remediation efforts and communicate risk levels clearly across teams and organizations.

The CVSS score is derived from three metric groups: base, temporal, and environmental. The base metrics represent the intrinsic characteristics of a vulnerability that are constant over time and across user environments. These include factors such as attack vector, attack complexity, privileges required, user interaction, scope, and the impacts on confidentiality, integrity, and availability. For example, a vulnerability that can be exploited remotely over the internet without authentication, with high impact on system availability, would receive a higher base score than one that requires local access and has a minimal impact.

The temporal metrics account for the characteristics of a vulnerability that may change over time but are independent of specific environments. These include the availability of exploit code, the level of remediation available, and the degree of confidence in the vulnerability's technical details. A vulnerability with mature exploit code that is easy to use would receive a higher temporal score than one with no known exploitation methods. Temporal metrics help refine prioritization based on current threat intelligence and exploit development trends, making the score more relevant in real-time decision-making.

The environmental metrics adjust the base and temporal scores to reflect the specific characteristics of the affected environment. These metrics include factors such as the importance of the affected asset, the potential collateral damage, and the presence of mitigating controls. For instance, if a vulnerability affects a system that is isolated from the internet and contains no sensitive data, its environmental score might be lower than the base score would suggest. Conversely, if the same vulnerability impacts a mission-critical server that holds customer information, the environmental score may increase significantly. Customizing CVSS scores with environmental inputs allows organizations to align scoring with business context and operational priorities.

The current version of the framework, CVSS v3.1, introduced refinements to address limitations found in earlier versions. For example, the scope metric was added to reflect whether a vulnerability can affect other components beyond its immediate environment, improving the accuracy of impact assessments. Additionally, the distinction between attack complexity and privileges required was clarified to offer more granularity in determining how difficult it is for an attacker to exploit a given vulnerability. These improvements make CVSS more effective as a scoring methodology, although it still requires interpretation and contextualization to guide real-world actions.

Despite its usefulness, CVSS is not without criticism. One of the main challenges is that it does not provide insight into the likelihood of exploitation in the wild. A vulnerability may receive a high CVSS score due to its theoretical severity, but if there is no exploit code available or if it is impractical to exploit, the real-world risk may be low.

Conversely, a vulnerability with a medium score might be actively exploited by ransomware groups, making it far more urgent than its numerical score would suggest. This is why many organizations supplement CVSS with threat intelligence feeds and exploitability data to improve the accuracy of their prioritization.

Another common issue with CVSS is score inflation, especially when vulnerability disclosures focus heavily on the base score. Vendors and researchers may highlight the maximum possible severity of a vulnerability without accounting for environmental or temporal factors, which can lead to exaggerated perceptions of risk. Security teams must resist the temptation to rely solely on high scores as indicators of priority and must instead assess the full context of each vulnerability. This includes reviewing the exploitability, the location and role of the affected asset, the presence of compensating controls, and the potential business impact of exploitation.

Additionally, the manual effort required to apply environmental metrics accurately can limit the practical use of CVSS in large-scale environments. Many vulnerability management systems report only the base score by default, as it is readily available from public vulnerability databases. To use the full power of CVSS, organizations need to invest in processes and tools that allow them to apply environmental metrics in an automated or semi-automated manner. This can involve tagging assets with business value indicators, integrating CVSS calculations with asset inventories, and using orchestration tools to enrich vulnerability data with contextual information.

CVSS remains an indispensable tool in the vulnerability management toolkit, providing a structured way to evaluate and communicate the potential impact of security flaws. It offers a common language that bridges the gap between security experts, developers, operations staff, and business stakeholders. However, it should be seen as a starting point rather than a definitive guide. When combined with other data sources, such as exploitability trends, asset criticality, compliance requirements, and operational constraints, CVSS becomes part of a comprehensive approach to risk-based vulnerability management.

Understanding the mechanics and nuances of CVSS enables security teams to make better-informed decisions. It allows for consistent scoring across diverse systems and fosters transparency in how vulnerabilities are assessed. It also supports the development of automated workflows for prioritization, reporting, and compliance. By using CVSS not in isolation but in conjunction with broader risk management strategies, organizations can ensure that their response to vulnerabilities is both timely and aligned with the realities of their environment. The framework's value lies in its adaptability, its clarity, and its capacity to support scalable and strategic security practices across the enterprise.

Vulnerability Databases and Feeds

Vulnerability databases and feeds form the backbone of any modern vulnerability management program. They provide the raw data necessary for identifying known security weaknesses across software, hardware, and firmware. These sources serve as repositories of vulnerability information, collecting data from vendors, researchers, cybersecurity organizations, and threat intelligence groups. Without access to accurate and up-to-date vulnerability data, organizations would be unable to detect, assess, or remediate the risks present in their environments. These databases not only list vulnerabilities but often provide detailed metadata such as severity scores, affected versions, references, exploit availability, and patch information, enabling security professionals to make informed decisions based on reliable intelligence.

The most widely known and used vulnerability database is the National Vulnerability Database, maintained by the National Institute of Standards and Technology in the United States. The NVD is built upon the Common Vulnerabilities and Exposures system, which assigns unique identifiers to publicly known vulnerabilities. These CVE identifiers standardize vulnerability references across vendors and tools, allowing different systems to share consistent data. The NVD enriches CVE entries with additional metadata, including CVSS scores, impact metrics, solution references, and affected products. Because of its open and comprehensive nature, the NVD is commonly integrated into vulnerability scanners, security dashboards, and asset management systems, forming a centralized source of truth for known vulnerabilities.

In addition to the NVD, many organizations rely on proprietary vulnerability databases maintained by commercial security vendors. These databases often include zero-day vulnerabilities, advanced threat intelligence, exploit indicators, and product-specific guidance that may not be immediately available in public sources. Vendors such as Qualys, Tenable, Rapid7, and IBM maintain their own vulnerability knowledge bases, offering customers real-time updates and tailored intelligence that enhances their ability to respond quickly. These proprietary feeds often prioritize timely updates, accuracy, and contextual insights, filling in the gaps that public sources may leave. For organizations with critical infrastructure, sensitive data, or high compliance requirements, access to premium vulnerability feeds can provide a critical advantage.

Another important category of vulnerability feeds includes vendor-specific advisories. Software and hardware manufacturers regularly publish security bulletins when vulnerabilities are discovered in their products. These advisories may be hosted on dedicated security portals or distributed via email lists and APIs. Unlike centralized databases, vendor advisories often contain highly detailed, product-specific information, including exact version numbers, affected modules, and platform nuances. They may also include recommended configuration changes, temporary mitigations, and links to software updates. Monitoring these advisories is essential for maintaining a current understanding of vulnerabilities within the organization's deployed technology stack, especially when relying on niche or proprietary systems.

Community-driven vulnerability feeds and open-source intelligence also play an important role. Projects like the Open Source Vulnerability Database, Vulners, and Exploit-DB collect and share vulnerability information, often including exploit code and proof-of-concept scripts. These sources contribute to transparency and knowledge sharing within the security community, providing practical insights into how vulnerabilities are discovered and weaponized. While these feeds may vary in reliability and curation quality, they offer a valuable perspective on vulnerabilities from the research and offensive security communities. Organizations that monitor these sources can gain early warnings of threats and a better understanding of how attackers operate.

Timeliness is a key factor in evaluating the usefulness of a vulnerability feed. The faster a vulnerability is reported, verified, and distributed, the sooner it can be addressed. Delays in publication can leave organizations exposed to threats that are already being exploited in the wild. High-quality feeds are characterized by low latency between disclosure and distribution. This speed enables organizations to initiate internal scans, patch deployments, or compensating controls before adversaries can take advantage of the newly discovered weakness. Real-time or near-real-time feeds are especially valuable for zero-day threats and actively exploited vulnerabilities, where even hours of delay can have serious consequences.

Another critical aspect of vulnerability databases and feeds is their ability to provide actionable context. Raw vulnerability data is only useful when it can be understood and applied within the organization's environment. Actionable context includes information such as attack vectors, authentication requirements, system exposure, and known exploitation activity. Some feeds go further by including risk scoring that accounts for asset criticality, exploit maturity, and threat landscape relevance. This enriched data allows security teams to prioritize vulnerabilities not only by severity but by actual risk, focusing remediation efforts where they will have the greatest impact.

Effective use of vulnerability databases and feeds requires integration with internal systems. Most organizations utilize vulnerability management platforms, security information and event management systems, and configuration management tools to aggregate and act on external data. These integrations allow automated correlation between known vulnerabilities and the organization's asset inventory, providing a live view of exposure across the environment. Alerts can be generated automatically when a new vulnerability affects a critical asset, and remediation tasks can be assigned through ticketing systems. This automation reduces the burden on security teams and ensures that data from feeds is transformed into real-world action.

One of the challenges in managing multiple vulnerability feeds is avoiding redundancy and information overload. Many feeds contain overlapping data, and multiple reports on the same vulnerability can vary in terms of depth, accuracy, or severity assessments. Security teams must establish processes for de-duplication, validation, and enrichment of data from different sources. Advanced correlation engines and vulnerability intelligence platforms can assist in consolidating this information and presenting a unified, prioritized view. It is also important to continuously evaluate the quality and performance of each feed to ensure they remain aligned with the organization's evolving needs.

Language barriers, inconsistent formats, and lack of standardization across feeds also create operational friction. While CVE provides a global reference framework, not all vulnerability feeds use consistent identifiers or data models. Structured formats like JSON, STIX, and XML facilitate machine readability and integration, but feeds that use plain text or proprietary formats may require additional parsing and normalization. Investing in tools that can normalize and process feeds automatically helps reduce manual effort and enables broader adoption of diverse data sources.

Vulnerability databases and feeds are more than just repositories of data—they are living resources that reflect the evolving state of cybersecurity threats. Their effectiveness depends on the frequency of updates, the depth of information provided, the reliability of sources, and the ability of organizations to consume and act on their content. A mature vulnerability management program treats these feeds not as static references but as dynamic inputs that inform every stage of the security lifecycle. From detection and assessment to prioritization and remediation, they serve as the connective tissue between external threat intelligence and internal security operations, enabling organizations to respond to vulnerabilities with speed, precision, and confidence.

Zero-Day Vulnerabilities and How to React

Zero-day vulnerabilities represent one of the most dangerous and unpredictable threats in the cybersecurity landscape. These are flaws in software or hardware that are unknown to the vendor and, as a result, have no official patch or fix available at the time they are discovered or exploited. The term zero-day comes from the fact that developers have had zero days to address the vulnerability before it is exploited in the wild. The window of exposure for zero-day vulnerabilities is especially concerning because attackers can act without opposition, targeting systems before defenders are even aware of the weakness. In a world where cyberattacks have become increasingly sophisticated and well-funded, the ability to detect and respond to zero-day threats quickly is a critical measure of an organization's resilience.

What makes zero-day vulnerabilities particularly challenging is the lack of warning. Traditional vulnerability management processes rely on public disclosures, vulnerability feeds, and security advisories to identify weaknesses. In the case of a zero-day, none of these sources provide any insight because the flaw has not yet been publicly acknowledged. Often, it is the attackers who discover these vulnerabilities first, sometimes through independent research, but frequently through purchase from exploit brokers on the dark web or by conducting targeted testing on widely used systems. Once a zero-day is discovered and weaponized, it can be used to bypass defenses, install malware, exfiltrate data, or gain persistent access to critical systems without triggering traditional alarms.

Organizations cannot prevent zero-days from existing, but they can prepare for them. Preparation begins with implementing a strong security architecture that emphasizes defense in depth. Layers of protection such as firewalls, intrusion prevention systems, application controls, and network segmentation reduce the chance that a zero-day exploit will succeed in compromising critical systems. Since there is no immediate patch for a zero-day vulnerability, compensating controls become the first line of defense. These might include restricting unnecessary services, enforcing least privilege access, monitoring behavioral anomalies, and ensuring that endpoint protection systems are actively updated and tuned to detect suspicious activity.

When a zero-day is discovered, either through internal detection or external alert, speed becomes critical. The first step is identifying the scope of the exposure. Security teams must determine which systems are affected, what versions of software are in use, and whether there are any signs of active exploitation. Threat intelligence plays a vital role here. Even if the technical details of the vulnerability are not yet public, reputable intelligence sources may report on observed attacks, indicators of compromise, or the types of organizations being targeted. This information can guide the immediate response, helping defenders focus their efforts on the most vulnerable areas.

Containment is the next priority. If exploitation has been observed or is strongly suspected, systems may need to be taken offline, isolated, or heavily monitored. Logging and forensic analysis should be activated to collect evidence of any unauthorized access or manipulation. This data is critical for understanding the nature of the attack and for determining whether the breach is part of a larger campaign. At the same time, affected vendors should be contacted if they have not already issued an advisory. Vendors often work quickly to investigate and develop patches once they are made aware of a zero-day, especially if exploitation is ongoing.

In many cases, vendors will publish temporary mitigation steps before a formal patch is released. These might include configuration changes, disabling certain features, or applying access controls that reduce the risk of exploitation. Organizations must stay closely attuned to vendor updates, advisories, and security bulletins to implement these mitigations as soon as they become available. Waiting for a final patch can result in prolonged exposure, especially when threat actors are actively targeting the vulnerability. Temporary mitigations are not perfect, but they can significantly reduce the attack surface while buying time for a more permanent solution.

Communication across the organization is also critical during a zero-day event. Stakeholders from security, IT operations, legal, compliance, and executive leadership must be kept informed of the situation, the steps being taken, and any potential impact to services or customers. If the vulnerability affects customer-facing platforms or involves sensitive data, regulatory notification requirements may be triggered. Transparent and timely communication is essential for maintaining trust and avoiding legal or reputational consequences.

Once a patch becomes available, rapid testing and deployment are essential. However, organizations must still balance urgency with caution. Testing the patch in a controlled environment helps ensure that it does not disrupt operations or introduce new issues. In environments with large numbers of systems or complex dependencies, deploying patches quickly requires coordination and automation. Patch management tools and configuration management systems can assist in distributing updates and verifying successful application. Once the patch is fully deployed, systems should be rescanned and monitored to confirm that the vulnerability has been resolved.

After the immediate threat has been addressed, organizations must conduct a post-incident review. This review should analyze how the vulnerability was detected, how quickly the response unfolded, what tools or controls were most effective, and where gaps were identified. Lessons learned from a zero-day response can be used to refine policies, update incident response playbooks, and strengthen monitoring strategies. Over time, this process builds organizational muscle memory, making future responses faster and more effective.

In addition to reactive measures, proactive strategies can reduce the risk posed by zero-day vulnerabilities. Code auditing, vulnerability research, bug bounty programs, and red teaming exercises can uncover unknown vulnerabilities before they are discovered by adversaries. Working closely with software vendors, contributing to security research communities, and staying engaged with industry-specific threat intelligence groups can also improve awareness and readiness. While zero-day threats can never be entirely eliminated, a proactive and prepared organization can significantly reduce the impact they cause.

Zero-day vulnerabilities test every aspect of an organization's security readiness. They demand fast action, coordinated response, and the ability to operate with limited information. The organizations best equipped to handle zero-day incidents are those that have built a culture of preparedness, invested in layered defenses, and integrated threat intelligence into their daily operations. By treating zero-day vulnerabilities as a reality rather than a rare exception, and by planning accordingly, organizations can respond with resilience and precision when the unexpected occurs.

Vulnerability Disclosure Programs

Vulnerability disclosure programs have become a cornerstone of modern cybersecurity strategies. These programs provide structured processes for external security researchers, ethical hackers, and even internal stakeholders to report security vulnerabilities they discover in an organization's systems, applications, or infrastructure. The premise behind a disclosure program is rooted in transparency, collaboration, and continuous improvement. By encouraging the responsible reporting of vulnerabilities, organizations can identify and remediate security flaws before they are exploited maliciously, thereby reducing overall risk and demonstrating a commitment to security best practices.

At their core, vulnerability disclosure programs are about building a bridge between organizations and the security community. In the past, organizations often viewed unsolicited vulnerability reports with suspicion, sometimes even threatening legal action against researchers who disclosed issues without permission. This adversarial approach discouraged responsible reporting and often led to vulnerabilities being ignored or publicly exposed without a chance for remediation. In contrast, formal disclosure programs create a safe and respectful channel through which vulnerabilities can be submitted, evaluated, and addressed in a collaborative manner. This not only fosters goodwill but also brings valuable external perspectives into an organization's security ecosystem.

A well-designed vulnerability disclosure program outlines the rules of engagement for reporting. It typically includes clear instructions on how to submit a report, what information should be included, which systems or applications are in scope, and how the organization will respond. These details are often published in a disclosure policy hosted on the company's website. Transparency in the policy is crucial because it builds trust with the security community. Researchers need to know that their efforts will be acknowledged, that they will not face retaliation, and that the organization takes their findings seriously. Some programs also provide legal safe harbor statements, assuring researchers that they will not be prosecuted for ethical hacking activities conducted in good faith under the program's guidelines.

One of the key benefits of a disclosure program is the early detection of vulnerabilities that may have otherwise gone unnoticed. Security researchers use diverse techniques and tools to identify weaknesses, often approaching systems from unique angles that internal teams may not consider. Their independent assessments can uncover flaws in custom code, misconfigurations, outdated dependencies, and insecure integrations that evade automated scans. By opening a channel to these external experts, organizations effectively expand their security coverage without significantly increasing internal costs. This can lead to the discovery of critical vulnerabilities that, if left unaddressed, could result in data breaches, service disruptions, or regulatory violations.

Successful vulnerability disclosure programs also rely on robust internal processes. Once a report is received, it must be triaged and validated promptly. The triage process involves assessing the credibility of the report, reproducing the issue, determining its severity, and identifying affected assets. Timely and accurate triage ensures that critical vulnerabilities are prioritized and that researchers receive feedback on the status of their submissions. Communication during this phase is essential. Researchers should be acknowledged quickly and kept informed of progress. Even if a report is ultimately deemed to be low impact or out of scope, respectful communication helps maintain positive relationships with the security community and encourages future engagement.

Many organizations take their disclosure efforts a step further by offering incentives. While vulnerability disclosure programs are distinct from bug bounty programs, they can be a stepping stone toward them. A disclosure program may evolve to include monetary rewards, public recognition, or other forms of appreciation for high-quality findings. This motivates researchers to dedicate more time and effort to testing systems thoroughly and submitting detailed reports.

However, even without financial rewards, recognition such as a public hall of fame or certificates of appreciation can go a long way in encouraging participation. The key is to demonstrate that the organization values the contribution and is willing to act on it.

The integration of a disclosure program into the larger vulnerability management lifecycle is crucial for effectiveness. Reported vulnerabilities should enter the same workflows used for internally discovered issues, allowing for tracking, prioritization, remediation, and verification. Coordination between security, development, and operations teams is vital to ensure that fixes are implemented in a timely and controlled manner. Once remediation is complete, organizations should follow up with the reporting researcher, informing them of the outcome and, when appropriate, thanking them publicly. This reinforces the collaborative nature of the process and provides closure for all parties involved.

Regulatory and industry standards increasingly recognize the value of vulnerability disclosure programs. Frameworks such as ISO/IEC 29147 and guidelines from organizations like ENISA and the US Cybersecurity and Infrastructure Security Agency provide best practices for establishing and managing disclosure programs. In some sectors, such as finance and critical infrastructure, regulators may even require the implementation of formal disclosure channels. These trends reflect a growing consensus that openness and cooperation with the security community are essential components of a mature cybersecurity posture.

Despite their benefits, disclosure programs are not without challenges. Organizations must be prepared to handle a potentially high volume of submissions, some of which may be invalid, duplicate, or low quality. Establishing filtering mechanisms and clear criteria for in-scope vulnerabilities helps manage this workload. Another challenge is internal resistance. Some business units may be wary of exposing systems to scrutiny or may fear reputational damage from the public acknowledgment of vulnerabilities. Education and leadership support are key to overcoming this resistance and embedding the program into the organization's security culture.

The digital landscape is evolving rapidly, and vulnerabilities are an inevitable byproduct of complex systems and accelerated development cycles. In this context, vulnerability disclosure programs provide a proactive approach to identifying and fixing security flaws before they can be exploited. They signal to customers, partners, and regulators that the organization is committed to transparency, accountability, and continuous improvement. More importantly, they turn potential adversaries into allies, creating a community of defenders who work together to strengthen the digital ecosystem. As threats become more sophisticated, this collective vigilance becomes an indispensable part of staying secure. A well-run disclosure program is not just a technical process—it is a strategic asset that reflects the values of trust, collaboration, and resilience.

Role of Bug Bounties in Vulnerability Management

The role of bug bounties in vulnerability management has evolved significantly in recent years, becoming a powerful and strategic component of modern security programs. Bug bounty programs offer financial incentives to independent security researchers who discover and report vulnerabilities in an organization's systems, applications, or infrastructure. Unlike traditional penetration tests, which are typically time-bound and performed by a small group of consultants, bug bounty programs harness the collective expertise of a global community of ethical hackers. This crowdsourced model allows organizations to uncover more vulnerabilities, often with greater depth and diversity of perspective, enhancing the overall effectiveness of their vulnerability management efforts.

At the heart of any bug bounty program is the principle of incentivized transparency. By inviting external researchers to probe their systems in exchange for rewards, organizations openly acknowledge the reality that no system is perfectly secure. This proactive stance signals a willingness to engage with the broader security community and a commitment to continuous improvement. Bug bounty programs create a mutually beneficial relationship where researchers are rewarded for their efforts, and organizations benefit from early detection of vulnerabilities before they can be exploited by malicious actors.

The advantages of integrating bug bounties into a vulnerability management program are numerous. One of the most significant benefits is scale. With potentially hundreds or even thousands of researchers participating, bug bounty programs vastly increase the number of eyes analyzing a system. This scale leads to a higher likelihood of discovering subtle, complex, or high-impact vulnerabilities that might evade traditional testing methods. Participants in bug bounty programs often bring unique skills, experiences, and tools, which result in diverse testing methodologies. This diversity increases the probability of uncovering edge cases, logical flaws, and vulnerabilities in obscure components that automated scanners and in-house teams might miss.

Another key benefit is speed. Once a bug bounty program is launched, researchers begin testing almost immediately. Unlike scheduled assessments, bug bounty programs operate continuously, allowing for real-time identification of vulnerabilities as systems evolve. This is particularly valuable in agile development environments where new features, updates, and integrations are rolled out frequently. A continuous feedback loop with external researchers enables organizations to adapt quickly, address issues before attackers can exploit them, and maintain a more secure product lifecycle.

The financial model of bug bounty programs also promotes efficiency. Organizations only pay for results, meaning that rewards are issued only when valid vulnerabilities are discovered and verified. This outcome-based model ensures that budget allocations are directly tied to the value received. While setting appropriate reward tiers is important for attracting and retaining talented researchers, the cost-effectiveness of bug bounty programs compared to traditional assessments makes them appealing to organizations of all sizes. Small startups and large enterprises alike can tailor their programs based on available resources and risk tolerance.

However, running a successful bug bounty program requires careful planning and management. It begins with defining the scope of the program, which specifies what systems, applications, and components are eligible for testing. The scope should be clearly communicated, realistic, and aligned with the organization's ability to respond to reported vulnerabilities. Including too many assets without adequate internal support can overwhelm security teams, while too narrow a scope may fail to attract researchers. Additionally, defining severity thresholds, reward amounts, and response timelines sets expectations for both participants and internal stakeholders, reducing friction and promoting fairness.

Effective triage is another critical component of bug bounty program management. With the potential for high submission volumes, many of which may be duplicates or low quality, security teams must be prepared to validate findings quickly and accurately. Triage teams must assess the credibility of each submission, determine its impact, and initiate appropriate remediation processes. Communication with researchers is key during this stage, as delays or lack of transparency can lead to frustration and disengagement. Prompt responses, respectful feedback, and fair assessments build trust and encourage sustained participation from high-caliber researchers.

Integrating bug bounty findings into the broader vulnerability management workflow is essential for consistency and visibility. Validated reports should follow the same remediation, tracking, and verification processes as internally discovered vulnerabilities. This ensures accountability, avoids duplication of effort, and supports reporting requirements for compliance and risk assessment. Over time, analyzing data from bug bounty submissions can reveal patterns, such as recurring flaws in specific codebases, misconfigurations in certain environments, or gaps in developer training. These insights support root cause analysis and continuous improvement initiatives across the organization.

Bug bounty programs can also serve as valuable talent pipelines. Many organizations have recruited top-performing researchers from their programs into internal security roles. These individuals often bring deep technical expertise, practical experience, and a strong understanding of offensive security tactics. Involving internal teams in the management and review of bug bounty submissions also fosters skill development, encourages a culture of curiosity, and promotes cross-functional learning.

Despite their benefits, bug bounty programs are not a silver bullet. They complement, rather than replace, other vulnerability management practices such as code reviews, automated scanning, threat modeling, and formal assessments. Bug bounty programs are most effective when deployed as part of a layered security strategy that includes proactive and reactive components. Their success depends on the organization's maturity, its ability to process and respond to findings, and its openness to external collaboration.

Legal and ethical considerations must also be addressed. A strong bug bounty policy includes clear terms of engagement, safe harbor provisions, and guidelines for responsible disclosure. Legal teams should be involved in drafting these policies to protect both the organization and participating researchers. Avoiding ambiguous language, respecting the rights of ethical hackers, and fostering an environment of cooperation are all critical for building a reputable and sustainable program.

Public perception of bug bounty programs is increasingly positive. As major technology companies, financial institutions, and government agencies adopt these programs, the stigma once associated with external testing has diminished. Today, having a bug bounty program is often seen as a mark of maturity and forward-thinking security leadership. It demonstrates that an organization values openness, is committed to protecting its users, and is willing to engage constructively with the global security community.

The role of bug bounties in vulnerability management is to extend reach, increase resilience, and accelerate discovery in ways that internal teams alone cannot achieve. By embracing this model, organizations gain access to a vast pool of talent, enhance their ability to detect complex threats, and foster a culture of continuous security improvement. As digital systems become more interconnected and threats more sophisticated, the collaboration enabled through bug bounty programs will remain a powerful force in defending against vulnerabilities and building trust in technology.

Open Source Vulnerability Management

Open source vulnerability management has emerged as a vital discipline within cybersecurity, as organizations increasingly rely on open source software to power their digital infrastructure. From operating systems and web servers to programming libraries and container images, open source components form the backbone of modern software development. These components are often integrated into proprietary systems, used in critical environments, and trusted for performance and flexibility. However, with this widespread adoption comes significant risk, particularly when vulnerabilities are discovered in widely used open source projects. Managing these vulnerabilities requires visibility, strategy, and coordination across development, security, and operational teams.

One of the fundamental challenges of open source vulnerability management is that organizations often use far more open source components than they realize. Developers routinely incorporate libraries and packages from public repositories, many of which bring transitive dependencies—additional components required for the software to function. A single open source library might pull in dozens or even hundreds of indirect dependencies, each with their own potential vulnerabilities. Without a comprehensive inventory of all open source software in use, organizations lack the visibility needed to assess their exposure when new vulnerabilities are disclosed. This lack of awareness is one of the most significant blind spots in modern vulnerability management.

Software composition analysis, or SCA, tools are essential for addressing this visibility gap. These tools scan codebases, binaries, and build environments to identify all open source components and their versions. Once this information is collected, it is compared against public vulnerability databases to detect known security flaws. This automated approach allows organizations to track their open source usage at scale and receive timely alerts when new vulnerabilities are discovered in the components they depend on. The ability to continuously monitor open source software is critical because new vulnerabilities are disclosed regularly, and previously benign components can suddenly become high-risk.

Managing vulnerabilities in open source software differs from managing proprietary software in several ways. First, responsibility for patching is decentralized. While vendors typically provide patches for proprietary products through structured release cycles, open source projects vary widely in terms of their responsiveness, resources, and governance. Some well-maintained projects release security updates quickly and maintain detailed advisories, while others may lack formal security processes altogether. In some cases, there may be no official maintainer available to fix a critical vulnerability. This variability makes it necessary for organizations to not only monitor for vulnerabilities but also assess the health and maturity of the open source projects they use.

When a vulnerability is discovered in an open source component, the remediation process typically involves updating to a secure version. However, this is not always straightforward. Upgrading a dependency may introduce breaking changes, require application refactoring, or impact compatibility with other components. Security teams must work closely with development teams to evaluate the feasibility and impact of each update. Automated dependency management tools, such as those integrated into CI/CD pipelines, can help streamline this process by suggesting and testing updates before they are merged. Still, prioritization is key. Not every vulnerability requires immediate action, and decisions must be based on factors such as severity, exploitability, asset criticality, and application exposure.

Another complication arises from the sheer volume of vulnerabilities disclosed each year. Open source components often receive vulnerability disclosures that, while technically valid, may not apply to every use case. For example, a vulnerability in a function that is not invoked by the application, or one that requires conditions that are not present in the deployment environment, may pose minimal risk. Understanding how a component is used in context is essential to avoid unnecessary updates and to focus remediation efforts where they matter most. This requires input from developers who understand the code and from security analysts who can interpret the threat.

Open source vulnerability management also involves supply chain risk. Attackers increasingly target the software supply chain by injecting malicious code into open source projects, compromising repositories, or publishing counterfeit packages with similar names. These supply chain attacks bypass traditional perimeter defenses and exploit the trust placed in public ecosystems. Preventing such attacks involves not only scanning for known vulnerabilities but also validating the integrity and origin of software components. Practices such as code signing, checksum verification, and the use of vetted repositories can help ensure that open source components are authentic and untampered.

Collaboration with the open source community is another important aspect of effective vulnerability management. When organizations discover vulnerabilities in open source projects, responsible disclosure to the maintainers is essential. Contributing patches, participating in security discussions, and supporting open source maintainers financially or through code contributions strengthens the security of the ecosystem as a whole. Many organizations also benefit from participating in foundations or initiatives focused on improving open source security practices, such as the Open Source Security Foundation (OpenSSF). These collaborations foster shared responsibility and drive improvements in tooling, standards, and awareness.

Policy and governance play a critical role in managing open source risk. Organizations must establish clear guidelines for evaluating, selecting, and maintaining open source components. This includes defining acceptable licenses, vetting new dependencies before they are added to production systems, and periodically reviewing existing components for risk. Security champions within development teams can help promote secure usage of open source by conducting code reviews, promoting best practices, and facilitating communication between developers and security teams. A well-defined policy ensures that security is embedded into the software development lifecycle rather than treated as an afterthought.

Metrics and reporting support continuous improvement in open source vulnerability management. Organizations should track the number of open source components in use, the percentage with known vulnerabilities, the average time to remediation, and the rate of update adoption. These metrics provide insight into the effectiveness of security practices and help justify investments in automation, training, and tooling. Visibility into open source risk at the organizational level supports strategic decision-making and aligns security goals with business objectives.

The increasing reliance on open source software in every industry makes vulnerability management in this space more important than ever. With open source comes immense innovation and agility, but also the responsibility to manage risk proactively. By combining automation, collaboration, policy, and continuous monitoring, organizations can effectively identify and remediate vulnerabilities in open source software. They can also contribute to a more secure digital ecosystem, where transparency, community, and shared responsibility drive resilience and trust. The challenges are significant, but so too are the opportunities to build a more robust and secure foundation for the software that powers the modern world.

Cloud-Specific Vulnerabilities

Cloud-specific vulnerabilities represent a distinct and rapidly evolving category of security challenges in today's digital infrastructure. As organizations migrate workloads to the cloud for scalability, flexibility, and cost savings, they also expose themselves to new types of risks that differ significantly from those found in traditional on-premises environments. The cloud changes how resources are provisioned, accessed, and managed, and these changes introduce vulnerabilities that are unique to cloud platforms, particularly those arising from misconfigurations, identity management flaws, and the complex interplay of shared responsibility between cloud service providers and customers.

One of the most common and dangerous types of cloud-specific vulnerabilities stems from misconfigurations. Unlike traditional infrastructure, where network and system settings are often configured manually and follow well-established patterns, cloud environments rely heavily on declarative templates, APIs, and dynamic resource creation. As a result, it is easier for human error or oversight to result in overly permissive access policies, exposed storage buckets, or publicly reachable services that were not intended to be accessible. For example, a misconfigured Amazon S3 bucket set to public read access can inadvertently expose sensitive data to anyone with the URL. Similarly, improperly configured security groups in platforms like AWS or Azure can leave virtual machines or containers exposed to the internet with no authentication or logging.

Cloud misconfigurations are especially dangerous because they are difficult to detect without continuous monitoring and specialized tools. Unlike known software vulnerabilities, which can be identified using scanners and matched to CVE databases, misconfigurations require context-aware analysis. Organizations need to understand the intended architecture, policies, and data flows of their cloud environments to determine whether a given configuration constitutes a vulnerability. Tools designed for cloud security posture management (CSPM) play a critical role in this process by assessing configurations against best practices, compliance frameworks, and organizational policies, flagging deviations that may pose risk.

Another major source of cloud-specific vulnerabilities involves identity and access management (IAM). In cloud platforms, access to nearly every resource is governed by IAM policies, which define who can do what on which resources. Poorly written or overly permissive IAM policies can grant excessive privileges, creating opportunities for attackers to escalate their access or move laterally within the environment. For instance, a policy that grants full administrative access to multiple roles, even when only read-only permissions are required, increases the blast radius of any compromised credential. Additionally, failure to implement strong authentication mechanisms such as multi-factor authentication (MFA) can make it easier for attackers to exploit stolen credentials.

Credential exposure is a particular concern in cloud environments because of the prevalence of programmatic access through APIs, automation tools, and Infrastructure-as-Code templates. Developers may accidentally commit access keys, secrets, or tokens to public repositories or store them in plaintext in configuration files. Once exposed, these credentials can be harvested and used to perform unauthorized actions in the cloud environment. Cloud service providers offer tools such as secret managers and IAM roles to securely manage and rotate credentials, but organizations must adopt these tools consistently and correctly. Regular secret scanning and automated alerts for credential misuse are essential controls in reducing this risk.

The complexity and scale of cloud environments also introduce vulnerabilities through inter-service relationships and third-party integrations. Cloud-native applications often consist of dozens of interconnected services, including databases, message queues, serverless functions, and storage resources. These components must communicate securely, and any misconfigured trust relationship or over-permissioned role can open a path for attackers to traverse multiple services. Additionally, cloud services are frequently integrated with third-party platforms and tools via APIs, creating additional points of exposure. If these integrations are not properly authenticated, encrypted, and monitored, they can become entry points for supply chain attacks or data exfiltration.

One of the unique aspects of cloud computing is the concept of the shared responsibility model. This model defines the division of security responsibilities between the cloud service provider and the customer. While providers like AWS, Azure, and Google Cloud are responsible for securing the underlying infrastructure, including hardware, storage, and network, the customer is responsible for securing their own data, applications, and configurations. Misunderstanding this division of responsibility can lead to gaps in security coverage. Customers may assume that certain protections are in place by default, only to find that services were not configured securely or that logging and monitoring were not enabled.

Lack of visibility is a recurring challenge in cloud vulnerability management. Unlike traditional networks where system administrators have physical access and can deploy endpoint agents directly, cloud environments often abstract away infrastructure details. This abstraction limits visibility into underlying resources and can complicate the process of detecting and responding to threats. Cloud-native logging tools such as AWS CloudTrail, Azure Monitor, and Google Cloud Audit Logs provide valuable telemetry, but these tools must be explicitly enabled, configured, and integrated into a broader security operations workflow. Without proper logging and alerting, organizations may remain unaware of anomalous activity or policy violations until a breach occurs.

Data protection in the cloud also introduces unique concerns. Data stored in cloud environments is often distributed across multiple geographic regions and services, and without proper controls, sensitive data can be inadvertently shared, leaked, or replicated into insecure environments. Encryption at rest and in transit is a baseline requirement, but equally important is managing data access policies, auditing data usage, and preventing unauthorized transfers. Services like data loss prevention (DLP), storage access monitoring, and classification tools help organizations protect sensitive data and meet compliance obligations.

Automation, while a powerful enabler of cloud scalability, also introduces potential vulnerabilities when not properly governed. Automated scripts, orchestration tools, and CI/CD pipelines can propagate insecure configurations or outdated dependencies at scale. A single misstep in an automation script can introduce vulnerabilities across hundreds of instances within seconds. Securing automation requires embedding security checks into the development and deployment process, often through DevSecOps practices. This includes automated scanning for vulnerabilities in container images, policy enforcement for Infrastructure-as-Code templates, and continuous validation of deployment pipelines.

Cloud-specific vulnerabilities are not limited to infrastructure as a service (IaaS) environments. Platform as a service (PaaS) and software as a service (SaaS) offerings come with their own sets of risks. In PaaS environments, application-level security becomes even more important, as the underlying operating system is abstracted away. Misconfigurations in application frameworks, insecure use of managed databases, or exposed APIs can create significant risk. In SaaS environments, configuration errors in user permissions, sharing settings, and third-party app integrations can result in data exposure or account compromise.

Managing cloud-specific vulnerabilities requires a shift in mindset. Traditional perimeter-based models are no longer sufficient, and organizations must embrace continuous monitoring, dynamic policy enforcement, and automated remediation. Collaboration between cloud architects, developers, and security teams is essential to embed security into every layer of the cloud stack. As cloud adoption continues to grow, so too must the maturity of the tools, processes, and expertise required to secure it. Organizations that take a proactive and integrated approach to managing cloud-specific vulnerabilities will be better equipped to handle the complexity and pace of change that defines the cloud era.

Container Security and Vulnerability Handling

Container security and vulnerability handling have become crucial components of modern cybersecurity practices due to the widespread adoption of containerized architectures in cloud-native applications. Containers offer significant benefits in terms of portability, scalability, and deployment speed. However, they also introduce new challenges and risks that traditional security models are not well equipped to handle. Understanding the unique nature of containers and developing strategies to manage their vulnerabilities effectively is essential for any organization that relies on this technology to power its digital infrastructure.

Containers are lightweight, executable units that package application code along with all its dependencies, libraries, and configurations. Unlike virtual machines, which include an entire operating system, containers share the host OS kernel and run in isolated user spaces. This shared-kernel model enhances efficiency but also amplifies the consequences of misconfiguration or compromise. If a container escapes its isolated environment due to a vulnerability, it can potentially affect the host system or other containers running on the same host. This makes isolation, minimalism, and continuous monitoring essential principles in securing container environments.

One of the primary concerns in container security is the use of vulnerable base images. Developers frequently build containers using publicly available images from repositories like Docker Hub. These images may contain outdated software, unpatched vulnerabilities, or unnecessary components that increase the attack surface. Without careful scrutiny, these base images can introduce critical vulnerabilities into production environments. Organizations must establish policies for approved base images and enforce regular scanning of all images using tools designed for container vulnerability assessment. These tools inspect the layers of container images, compare them to known vulnerability databases, and flag any components that need to be updated or replaced.

Vulnerability scanning should be integrated into every stage of the container lifecycle, from development and testing to deployment and runtime. This approach is often referred to as shift-left security, meaning that security checks are performed early in the development pipeline rather than after deployment. Integrating vulnerability scanners into continuous integration and continuous deployment (CI/CD) pipelines enables automated detection and blocking of vulnerable images before they are pushed to production. This proactive strategy not only reduces the time to remediation but also minimizes the cost and effort associated with fixing issues later in the software delivery cycle.

In addition to scanning images for known vulnerabilities, organizations must manage secrets and credentials securely within containers. Hardcoding secrets such as API keys, database passwords, or access tokens into container images is a common mistake that can lead to severe security breaches. Once embedded in an image, these secrets can be extracted by anyone with access to the container. Secure handling of secrets involves using secret management tools, such as HashiCorp Vault, AWS Secrets Manager, or Kubernetes Secrets, which allow secrets to be injected into containers at runtime without being stored in the image itself. Proper access control, encryption, and auditing of secret usage are essential to preventing unauthorized access.

Another important aspect of container vulnerability handling is maintaining minimal and immutable containers. Minimal containers contain only the components necessary for the application to run, reducing the attack surface by eliminating unused packages and libraries. Immutable containers are built once and never modified after deployment. Any changes require building and deploying a new version. This practice enforces consistency, simplifies debugging, and ensures that known vulnerabilities are not introduced through ad hoc changes or configuration drift. By keeping containers minimal and immutable, organizations reduce the complexity of vulnerability management and improve the reliability of their environments.

Runtime security is a critical layer of container protection. Even with rigorous scanning and secure image creation, containers may still be compromised due to new vulnerabilities or runtime exploits. Monitoring container behavior in real time helps detect anomalous activities, such as unexpected network connections, privilege escalation attempts, or changes to the container file system. Tools like Falco, Sysdig, and other container-aware monitoring solutions can enforce runtime policies and alert administrators to suspicious behavior. These tools are designed to work with container orchestration platforms like Kubernetes and can integrate into existing security operations workflows to provide visibility and control.

Kubernetes, as the dominant container orchestration platform, introduces additional considerations for vulnerability management. Misconfigured Kubernetes settings can expose containers to unnecessary risk. For example, allowing containers to run as root, enabling privileged mode, or using overly permissive network policies can lead to serious vulnerabilities. Security controls such as role-based access control (RBAC), network segmentation, pod security policies, and admission controllers must be configured carefully to ensure that the Kubernetes environment enforces least privilege and separation of duties. Tools like kube-bench and kube-hunter help audit Kubernetes configurations against security benchmarks and identify areas that require hardening.

Container registries also play a key role in security. These registries store container images and serve as the source of truth during deployments. Organizations should use private, access-controlled registries to store their approved and scanned images. Public registries, while convenient, may lack the governance and security controls needed for production environments. Scanning images within registries and maintaining metadata about image provenance, build processes, and associated vulnerabilities enable better risk assessment and incident response. Version control of images and the ability to roll back to known-good versions are additional capabilities that support secure operations.

Patch management in container environments is handled differently than in traditional systems. Since containers are often immutable, applying patches involves rebuilding the image with updated components and redeploying it. This means that the responsibility for patching lies primarily with the development and DevOps teams rather than traditional IT operations. Establishing a regular cadence for image rebuilding, leveraging automated dependency updates, and maintaining visibility into base image updates from upstream sources are essential practices. Organizations must ensure that their pipelines include mechanisms for quickly incorporating security patches into container images and verifying the success of the deployment.

Security in containerized environments is a shared responsibility that spans development, operations, and security teams. Developers must build secure images, operations teams must ensure secure deployment and orchestration, and security teams must provide tools, policies, and oversight to detect and respond to threats. Achieving this collaboration requires a cultural shift towards DevSecOps, where security is embedded in every phase of the container lifecycle. Training, process alignment, and shared accountability are key enablers of this model.

The dynamic and distributed nature of containers introduces both opportunities and risks. Containers accelerate development and deployment, but they also demand new approaches to vulnerability management. By focusing on secure image creation, integrating scanning tools into CI/CD pipelines, enforcing runtime security policies, and hardening orchestration platforms, organizations can effectively manage vulnerabilities in container environments. This holistic approach ensures that the speed and agility offered by containers do not come at the expense of security and that modern applications can be deployed with confidence in their resilience against emerging threats.

Vulnerability Management in DevSecOps

Vulnerability management in DevSecOps represents a paradigm shift in how organizations approach application and infrastructure security. Traditionally, security was treated as a discrete stage that followed development and operations, often leading to delays, friction between teams, and vulnerabilities being discovered too late in the delivery pipeline. DevSecOps changes this by integrating security into every phase of the software development lifecycle, from initial design and coding to testing, deployment, and operations. This integration ensures that vulnerabilities are identified, addressed, and monitored continuously, enabling teams to deliver secure applications at the speed of modern business demands.

At the core of DevSecOps is the belief that security is a shared responsibility. Developers, operations engineers, and security professionals must collaborate closely, each bringing their expertise to build and maintain secure systems. For vulnerability management, this means breaking down the silos that traditionally separated security scans from development processes. Instead of treating vulnerability assessments as a post-deployment task, DevSecOps embeds them into the build and release pipelines. By doing so, vulnerabilities can be detected early, reducing the time and cost required to fix them and preventing insecure code from reaching production.

One of the most important practices in DevSecOps vulnerability management is the use of automated tools that scan code, dependencies, and configurations for known vulnerabilities. Static application security testing (SAST) tools analyze source code during development to identify potential flaws such as SQL injection, cross-site scripting, or buffer overflows. These tools integrate directly into development environments and version control systems, providing developers with real-time feedback and actionable insights. By catching issues as code is written, SAST helps shift security to the left, enabling developers to fix problems before they become deeply embedded in the application.

Dynamic application security testing (DAST) tools complement this approach by scanning running applications for vulnerabilities during the testing phase. These tools simulate real-world attacks on the application to detect issues such as authentication bypass, insecure cookies, and exposure of sensitive data. DAST is valuable because it assesses the application from the outside in, identifying vulnerabilities that may not be apparent in the code alone. In a DevSecOps environment, DAST scans are triggered automatically as part of the testing pipeline, ensuring that every build is evaluated for security risks before release.

Software composition analysis (SCA) is another essential tool in the DevSecOps toolkit. Modern applications rely heavily on third-party libraries, many of which contain known vulnerabilities. SCA tools inventory all dependencies used in a project, check their versions against vulnerability databases, and alert developers when insecure components are detected. These tools often provide detailed remediation guidance, including suggested upgrade paths and references to public advisories. Integrating SCA into the build process allows teams to maintain visibility over their supply chain and avoid introducing risk through outdated or untrusted packages.

Infrastructure-as-code (IaC) scanning is increasingly important in DevSecOps as infrastructure provisioning becomes automated. Tools that scan IaC templates, such as Terraform or CloudFormation files, can detect misconfigurations that may lead to vulnerable deployments. For example, an IaC template that provisions a publicly accessible database or disables encryption could expose sensitive data. By scanning these templates during code review and pipeline execution, teams can enforce security policies before the infrastructure is created. This prevents insecure environments from ever going live and reinforces a proactive security posture.

To make vulnerability management in DevSecOps successful, organizations must also establish a robust feedback loop. Security findings from tools and manual reviews must be communicated clearly and prioritized effectively. Not every vulnerability represents an immediate threat, and teams must be able to distinguish between critical risks and minor issues. Integrating vulnerability data with issue tracking systems allows findings to be assigned, tracked, and resolved within existing workflows. This reduces context switching and makes it easier for teams to manage technical debt related to security. Establishing service level objectives (SLOs) for remediation based on severity ensures that the most serious vulnerabilities are addressed promptly while still allowing development velocity to be maintained.

Cultural change is another fundamental aspect of DevSecOps vulnerability management. Developers must be empowered and educated to make secure choices, and security teams must act as enablers rather than gatekeepers. Providing training, playbooks, and automated security controls helps developers understand common vulnerabilities and how to avoid them. Encouraging collaboration through security champions—developers with security expertise embedded in each team—bridges knowledge gaps and fosters a culture of shared responsibility. When security is viewed as an integral part of quality, rather than a separate concern, the entire organization becomes more resilient to threats.

Metrics play a crucial role in measuring and improving vulnerability management within DevSecOps. Tracking the number of vulnerabilities discovered, the average time to remediation, and the percentage of builds blocked due to security issues provides visibility into the program's effectiveness. These metrics can be used to identify bottlenecks, optimize tooling, and demonstrate progress to stakeholders. Over time, they help refine processes and improve the maturity of security practices. Additionally, integrating security metrics with business outcomes, such as incident reduction or compliance adherence, helps justify investment in DevSecOps initiatives.

Tooling and automation alone are not enough. Governance and policy enforcement must be baked into the DevSecOps process. Security policies regarding code standards, dependency management, and deployment practices must be codified and enforced through policy-as-code. This approach ensures consistency and scalability across environments. Automated policy checks can prevent the deployment of artifacts that violate predefined rules, such as using deprecated libraries or exposing ports unnecessarily. By enforcing security policies automatically, teams can maintain speed while ensuring compliance with organizational and regulatory requirements.

In high-velocity environments, the ability to respond quickly to new vulnerabilities is paramount. Continuous monitoring and alerting systems must be in place to detect emerging threats, such as newly disclosed vulnerabilities in dependencies or configuration drift in cloud infrastructure. Integrating threat intelligence feeds with vulnerability scanning tools allows organizations to identify which assets are affected by high-profile vulnerabilities and initiate rapid response workflows. In cases of critical vulnerabilities, such as zero-days or supply chain compromises, automated workflows can trigger hotfix builds, notify stakeholders, and enforce temporary mitigations until a permanent solution is deployed.

Vulnerability management in DevSecOps is not a destination but an evolving journey. As threat landscapes shift and development practices advance, security processes must adapt. The integration of security into development and operations transforms vulnerability management from a reactive task into a continuous discipline. It enables organizations to scale securely, deliver value faster, and reduce the risk of security incidents. By embedding security into every phase of the lifecycle, DevSecOps ensures that vulnerability management becomes a natural and essential part of how software is built and maintained. This approach not only strengthens defenses but also empowers teams to innovate without compromising security.

Application Security Testing Integration

Application security testing integration is a foundational component of a comprehensive software security program. As modern development processes accelerate through agile methodologies and continuous integration and deployment pipelines, the need to embed security directly into the software development lifecycle has become paramount. Security testing must no longer be a siloed, end-of-cycle activity but an integrated, continuous function that evolves alongside the codebase. Integrating security testing into development workflows ensures that vulnerabilities are identified and addressed early, reduces remediation costs, and empowers developers to write more secure code without disrupting velocity.

One of the key pillars of application security testing integration is the adoption of static application security testing, or SAST. SAST tools analyze source code, bytecode, or binary code for vulnerabilities without executing the program. These tools detect issues such as hardcoded credentials, insecure data handling, injection flaws, and logic errors. When integrated into the development environment, SAST can provide real-time feedback to developers as they write code. This immediate insight helps prevent insecure coding practices and promotes security awareness among development teams. Embedding SAST into the continuous integration pipeline further ensures that each code commit is automatically analyzed, and builds can be blocked if critical issues are found.

Another essential aspect is dynamic application security testing, or DAST. DAST tools test running applications in a staging or test environment to uncover vulnerabilities in real-world conditions. These tools simulate attacks from an external perspective and are particularly effective at identifying issues such as broken authentication, insecure session management, and configuration errors. DAST is especially valuable for testing web applications, where user interaction and dynamic content can introduce complex security risks. By integrating DAST scans into automated testing pipelines, organizations can verify that deployed applications behave securely under normal and edge-case scenarios. DAST results complement SAST findings by revealing runtime vulnerabilities that may not be visible in the code.

Software composition analysis, or SCA, also plays a critical role in security testing integration. Applications today rely heavily on third-party components, libraries, and frameworks, many of which may contain known vulnerabilities. SCA tools inventory all dependencies, check their versions against public vulnerability databases, and alert development teams when insecure packages are used. These tools can also provide recommendations for safer alternatives and help manage license compliance. By integrating SCA into the build process, teams are alerted to security risks before the application is released, allowing them to update dependencies proactively and avoid introducing preventable vulnerabilities.

Interactive application security testing, or IAST, represents a hybrid approach that combines elements of both static and dynamic testing. IAST tools run inside the application during normal operation and monitor its behavior in real-time. This method provides detailed visibility into data flows, application logic, and runtime context, allowing for more accurate vulnerability detection with fewer false positives. IAST integration requires minimal disruption to development workflows and offers high-fidelity results that are directly actionable by developers. When deployed within test environments or during quality assurance stages, IAST tools can validate the effectiveness of fixes and detect security regressions introduced by code changes.

To maximize the effectiveness of application security testing integration, it is essential to automate testing within the existing development and deployment infrastructure. This includes triggering security scans on code commits, pull requests, and nightly builds, and providing results directly within developer tools such as integrated development environments or version control systems. Integration with ticketing systems, such as Jira or ServiceNow, enables security findings to be tracked, assigned, and resolved as part of the standard issue management process. Automating these steps reduces friction, ensures consistent testing coverage, and allows teams to address security issues as part of their normal workflow.

Security testing integration also demands a thoughtful approach to prioritization and noise reduction. Developers often face a high volume of alerts, many of which may be informational or irrelevant to the current context. To maintain productivity and avoid alert fatigue, security tools must provide accurate, context-rich findings and support customization of thresholds based on risk tolerance. Results should be mapped to standards such as OWASP Top Ten, CWE, or organizational policies to provide meaningful context. Tools that offer clear remediation guidance, including code snippets, links to documentation, and explanations of impact, help developers understand and resolve issues more efficiently.

Training and awareness are essential to the success of application security testing integration. Developers must be equipped not only with tools but with the knowledge to interpret and act on security findings. Integrating secure coding education, gamified challenges, and real-world examples into the development process builds a security-first mindset. Encouraging developers to participate in code reviews focused on security, and recognizing their contributions to reducing vulnerabilities, further reinforces this culture. Security champions programs, in which experienced developers serve as security advocates within their teams, can also bridge the gap between development and security disciplines.

Monitoring and metrics provide insight into the effectiveness of application security testing integration. Tracking the number and severity of vulnerabilities identified, the average time to remediation, and the percentage of builds passing security gates enables continuous improvement. These metrics can highlight trends, reveal bottlenecks, and support resource planning. Correlating security data with release velocity, incident frequency, and customer impact helps demonstrate the business value of integrated security testing and guides strategic investment.

Finally, application security testing integration must be adaptable and scalable. As development environments change, new programming languages are adopted, and architectures evolve toward microservices and serverless functions, security testing must keep pace. Tools must support a wide range of technologies and deployment models while maintaining performance and accuracy. Integration with container scanning, API security testing, and cloud configuration validation extends the reach of application security programs and provides comprehensive coverage across the software stack.

By embedding security testing into every stage of the development lifecycle, organizations gain the ability to identify and fix vulnerabilities early, reduce security debt, and foster collaboration between security and engineering teams. This integration transforms security from a barrier into an enabler, supporting innovation while protecting applications from threats. Application security testing integration is not just a technical challenge but a strategic imperative that requires alignment of people, processes, and tools. When executed effectively, it ensures that security becomes an inherent and seamless part of software development, strengthening trust, resilience, and agility in an increasingly complex digital landscape.

Endpoint Vulnerability Management

Endpoint vulnerability management plays a critical role in an organization's overall security posture, serving as a frontline defense against threats that originate from user devices such as laptops, desktops, mobile phones, and tablets. These endpoints are often the most exposed and most frequently targeted assets in any network. They are used by employees to access corporate data, applications, and systems, and they regularly interact with external environments that may not be secure. Because of this, endpoints represent a significant attack surface, and without a robust vulnerability management strategy, they can easily become entry points for malicious actors.

Managing vulnerabilities on endpoints involves a continuous cycle of discovery, assessment, prioritization, remediation, and verification. The first step is gaining visibility into all endpoint assets across the organization. This includes identifying the operating system, software versions, hardware configurations, and network connections of each device. Asset discovery tools and endpoint detection and response solutions are commonly used to build and maintain this inventory. Without a comprehensive understanding of what devices exist and what software they run, it is impossible to assess their security state accurately or determine where vulnerabilities lie.

Once endpoints are identified, the next step is to scan them for known vulnerabilities. This is typically done using vulnerability scanners that query endpoints for unpatched software, outdated drivers, insecure configurations, and other common weaknesses. Scanners compare the collected data against constantly updated vulnerability databases, such as the Common Vulnerabilities and Exposures list, to detect matching flaws. These scans should be conducted regularly to ensure new vulnerabilities are discovered quickly as they emerge. Endpoint scanning can be performed with agent-based solutions, where a small program runs on the device and reports data back to a central system, or agentless approaches that rely on remote access protocols. Each method has its benefits and drawbacks, but agent-based scanning usually provides more detailed visibility and control.

Prioritization is a fundamental part of effective endpoint vulnerability management. Not every vulnerability on every endpoint poses an immediate or serious threat. Factors such as the severity of the vulnerability, the exploitability in the wild, the sensitivity of data on the device, the user's privileges, and the endpoint's network exposure must all be considered. A critical vulnerability on an executive's laptop with access to sensitive financial data may take precedence over the same vulnerability on a shared kiosk with minimal privileges and no access to sensitive resources. Incorporating threat intelligence, risk scores, and business context into the prioritization process allows organizations to address the most dangerous vulnerabilities first, making the best use of limited remediation resources.

Remediation typically involves patching software, updating configurations, or removing unnecessary or vulnerable applications. This process can be complex, especially in environments with diverse operating systems, applications, and user needs. Automated patch management tools help streamline remediation by applying updates centrally and ensuring consistency across the endpoint fleet. These tools can schedule patches during maintenance windows, test compatibility before deployment, and roll back changes if issues are detected. Despite automation, patching can still be delayed by business constraints, compatibility concerns, or user resistance. In such cases, organizations should consider compensating controls, such as endpoint firewalls, application whitelisting, or network segmentation, to reduce risk until full remediation is possible.

Verification is an essential, yet often overlooked, phase of the vulnerability management cycle. After patches or other remediations are applied, follow-up scans must confirm that vulnerabilities have been successfully resolved. In some cases, patches may fail to install properly, users may revert changes, or new issues may arise as a result of the fix. Verification ensures that remediation efforts achieve their intended effect and provides an audit trail for compliance purposes. Regular reporting and metrics help track the effectiveness of the endpoint vulnerability management program and identify areas that need improvement.

Endpoint vulnerability management must also account for the growing trend of remote and hybrid work. With more employees working from home or using personal devices to access corporate systems, the traditional network perimeter has dissolved. Endpoints are now operating in less controlled environments, often outside of the reach of traditional network security tools. This shift makes it even more important to manage vulnerabilities directly at the endpoint level. Solutions that support remote patching, cloud-based vulnerability assessments, and integration with mobile device management platforms provide the flexibility needed to secure a decentralized workforce.

Security awareness and user behavior are also integral to managing endpoint vulnerabilities. Users often introduce risk by installing unauthorized applications, delaying system updates, or falling for phishing attacks that install malicious software. Educating users about secure practices, restricting administrative privileges, and enforcing security policies through endpoint protection platforms helps reduce the likelihood that vulnerabilities will be exploited. Additionally, endpoint detection and response tools provide real-time monitoring and automated response capabilities to detect and contain threats before they cause significant damage.

Another important aspect is endpoint diversity. In most organizations, endpoints vary widely in terms of operating systems, hardware configurations, and use cases. Managing vulnerabilities across Windows, macOS, Linux, Android, and iOS devices requires tools that can handle this heterogeneity. Each platform has unique vulnerabilities and patching mechanisms, and some may be more challenging to manage due to limited vendor support or restricted user access. Ensuring coverage across all types of endpoints requires careful planning, standardized configurations, and a layered security strategy.

Regulatory compliance also drives the need for strong endpoint vulnerability management. Many frameworks, such as HIPAA, PCI DSS, and GDPR, require organizations to demonstrate that they are actively managing and mitigating endpoint vulnerabilities. This includes documenting processes, maintaining up-to-date systems, and proving that identified vulnerabilities are remediated within defined timeframes. Failure to comply with these requirements can result in fines, legal consequences, and reputational damage. An effective endpoint vulnerability management program not only strengthens security but also supports the organization's compliance efforts.

In a threat landscape where attackers frequently target endpoints as the weakest link, managing their vulnerabilities is not optional. It is a continuous, dynamic process that requires visibility, automation, collaboration, and commitment. By investing in the right tools, aligning processes with business needs, and fostering a culture of security awareness, organizations can reduce their exposure and improve their ability to defend against modern threats. Endpoint vulnerability management is a foundational layer of defense that enables organizations to operate securely, adapt quickly to change, and build trust with users and stakeholders alike.

Vulnerability Management in OT and IoT

Vulnerability management in operational technology (OT) and Internet of Things (IoT) environments presents a unique and complex set of challenges that differ significantly from those in traditional IT infrastructures. OT systems control critical infrastructure, industrial machinery, and manufacturing processes, while IoT devices are embedded in everyday environments, from smart buildings and connected vehicles to medical devices and household appliances. Both types of systems are increasingly networked and internet-connected, expanding their functionality but also exposing them to cyber threats. As digital transformation integrates more of these devices into business operations and public services, the need for robust vulnerability management becomes urgent.

The foundational difficulty in managing vulnerabilities in OT and IoT systems lies in their design. Many OT and IoT devices were not originally built with cybersecurity in mind. They often run on proprietary or legacy operating systems, have limited processing power, and lack basic security features such as encryption, authentication, and remote update capabilities. Unlike traditional IT systems, these devices may operate in environments where availability and physical safety are prioritized over confidentiality or integrity. For example, in a power grid or a manufacturing plant, any disruption caused by a security update or misconfiguration can result in operational downtime, equipment damage, or even risk to human life.

This makes vulnerability remediation particularly delicate and time-sensitive.

Visibility is the first hurdle in OT and IoT vulnerability management. Organizations often lack an accurate inventory of all the devices operating in their environments. OT networks can include thousands of controllers, sensors, actuators, and human-machine interfaces that are difficult to track, especially when documentation is incomplete or vendors use proprietary protocols. Similarly, IoT environments may consist of numerous low-cost, consumer-grade devices that are deployed without centralized management. Without full visibility, identifying which devices are vulnerable is nearly impossible. Passive asset discovery tools that analyze network traffic are often used in OT settings to map devices without disrupting operations, while agentless scanning and specialized IoT management platforms help improve inventory in IoT networks.

Once visibility is achieved, the next step is assessing the vulnerabilities of these devices. Traditional vulnerability scanners used in IT environments are often unsuitable for OT and IoT systems. Active scans can disrupt fragile devices or flood networks with traffic they cannot handle. Instead, organizations rely on passive scanning, vendor advisories, and firmware analysis to detect vulnerabilities. In many cases, vulnerability data must be correlated manually with device models, firmware versions, and hardware configurations, as there is often no standardized naming or centralized database. The Common Vulnerabilities and Exposures (CVE) system is still evolving to better include OT and IoT vulnerabilities, but gaps remain in coverage, especially for proprietary systems and obscure vendors.

Prioritization of vulnerabilities in OT and IoT systems requires a deep understanding of operational context. Not all vulnerabilities are equal in these environments. A remote code execution flaw on a temperature sensor with no write capability may pose less risk than a privilege escalation vulnerability on a programmable logic controller that controls critical infrastructure. Asset criticality, physical proximity, potential for lateral movement, and safety implications must all be factored into risk assessments. Some OT environments operate under regulatory regimes that dictate specific risk thresholds and remediation timelines, such as those found in the energy and transportation sectors. In IoT environments, consumer safety and privacy laws increasingly demand responsible management of vulnerabilities, especially when personal data is involved.

Remediation in OT and IoT systems is one of the most challenging aspects of vulnerability management. Many devices do not support remote patching or automated updates. Even when updates are available, applying them may require taking equipment offline, which can be impractical or costly in continuous operations. In some cases, patches are not provided at all, especially for end-of-life devices or products from vendors with poor security support. Organizations must then rely on compensating controls, such as network segmentation, access control lists, and intrusion detection systems, to reduce the risk. In OT environments, the Purdue Model of network segmentation is often employed to isolate devices based on their role and risk profile. In IoT, techniques like microsegmentation and zero-trust architecture help limit exposure.

Vendor collaboration is a crucial component of effective vulnerability management in OT and IoT. Many vulnerabilities in these systems are discovered by external researchers or disclosed by vendors. Maintaining active relationships with manufacturers, participating in industry-specific information sharing forums, and subscribing to vendor advisories are necessary to stay informed. When vulnerabilities are identified, coordinated disclosure is essential. Vendors must be encouraged to produce patches and mitigations quickly, while users need sufficient guidance to deploy them safely. Public-private partnerships and regulatory frameworks are increasingly pushing vendors to adopt secure development practices and provide better long-term support for their products.

Monitoring and incident detection are also vital. Given the difficulty in patching, organizations must rely heavily on monitoring to detect exploitation attempts. Anomalous behavior, unexpected network communication, or deviations in process control logic may indicate a security breach. Specialized security tools such as industrial intrusion detection systems (IIDS) and security information and event management (SIEM) platforms configured for OT and IoT contexts are used to provide continuous visibility and alerting. These tools must be tuned carefully to avoid false positives and ensure compatibility with legacy systems. Monitoring data not only supports real-time defense but also feeds back into the vulnerability management process by highlighting which vulnerabilities are actively being exploited in the field.

Policy and governance frameworks support the institutionalization of OT and IoT vulnerability management. Organizations must establish clear policies for device onboarding, configuration, update management, and decommissioning. These policies should align with industry standards such as IEC 62443 for industrial cybersecurity or NIST's guidance for IoT security. Governance bodies must ensure that security is considered during procurement, that maintenance windows are planned with security updates in mind, and that responsibilities are clearly defined across security, engineering, and operational teams. A governance-driven approach ensures consistency, accountability, and continuous improvement in vulnerability management practices.

As the convergence of IT and OT accelerates, and as IoT devices become ubiquitous in both consumer and enterprise settings, the traditional boundaries of cybersecurity continue to blur. Vulnerabilities in a seemingly harmless IoT device or a misconfigured OT sensor can have cascading effects on data privacy, business continuity, and even physical safety. Organizations must therefore elevate OT and IoT security to the same strategic level as traditional IT security. Investing in visibility tools, building collaborative vendor relationships, adopting passive and non-intrusive assessment methods, and embedding security throughout the lifecycle of these devices are critical steps in achieving robust and sustainable vulnerability management in this expanding domain.

Penetration Testing as a Complement

Penetration testing, often referred to as ethical hacking, serves as a critical complement to traditional vulnerability management practices by providing a real-world perspective on how vulnerabilities could be exploited by adversaries. While automated tools and scanners are invaluable for identifying known vulnerabilities based on signatures and configurations, they cannot replicate the creativity, intuition, and adaptability of a skilled human attacker. Penetration testing bridges this gap by simulating attacks on systems, networks, and applications to uncover security weaknesses that may not be immediately apparent through automated assessments. This hands-on approach helps organizations not only validate their existing security controls but also understand the broader implications of risk across interconnected systems and processes.

The purpose of penetration testing is not just to identify vulnerabilities, but to demonstrate how they could be exploited in practice, what kind of access could be gained, and how far an attacker could go once initial access is achieved. This helps security teams prioritize remediation efforts based on real impact rather than theoretical severity. For example, an automated scanner might flag multiple vulnerabilities with high CVSS scores, but a penetration tester could show that one of those flaws, when combined with another seemingly low-severity issue, allows for complete system compromise. These insights are critical in environments where resources are limited, and decisions must be made quickly and strategically.

Penetration testing also uncovers misconfigurations, logic flaws, weak security practices, and other issues that may not be classified as formal vulnerabilities but still pose significant risk. These might include insecure authentication flows, poor session management, unvalidated input, or excessive user permissions. Such weaknesses often emerge from design oversights, integration complexities, or outdated assumptions about trust and access control. Because penetration testers think like attackers, they are well equipped to identify and exploit these flaws in a way that mimics real-world threat scenarios. This makes their findings highly relevant for improving the resilience of systems against advanced persistent threats and targeted attacks.

Unlike traditional vulnerability scans that cover large areas quickly and produce standardized reports, penetration testing is typically more focused and tailored. It may target a specific application, network segment, or business process, with the goal of simulating a particular type of attack. The scope of the engagement is defined in advance, and the testing methodology is aligned with industry standards such as the OWASP Testing Guide, NIST SP 800-115, or the PTES framework. This structured approach ensures consistency, repeatability, and compliance with legal and ethical guidelines. It also allows for clear communication of objectives, rules of engagement, and expected outcomes between the testing team and the organization.

There are several types of penetration tests, each serving a different purpose. External penetration testing focuses on internet-facing systems such as web servers, firewalls, and VPNs to assess how easily an outsider could gain unauthorized access. Internal penetration testing simulates an insider threat or an attacker who has already breached the perimeter and is moving laterally within the network. Web application penetration testing evaluates the security of custom-developed applications, APIs, and platforms for flaws such as injection, broken access controls, and insecure data storage. Wireless testing examines the security of wireless networks, devices, and communication protocols. Each of these test types contributes unique insights and reinforces other components of the security program.

Penetration testing is especially valuable when conducted regularly and integrated into broader security processes. Performing tests after major infrastructure changes, application launches, or compliance audits helps ensure that security remains aligned with evolving technology and business needs. Re-testing after vulnerabilities have been remediated verifies the effectiveness of fixes and ensures that no new issues have been introduced. Continuous or recurring penetration testing, sometimes called red teaming, provides an even deeper level of assessment by challenging the organization's detection and response capabilities. In these scenarios, testers often operate over extended periods with limited disclosure, simulating the behavior of real attackers to test the organization's readiness under pressure.

Another benefit of penetration testing is its ability to support regulatory and contractual compliance. Many frameworks and standards, such as PCI DSS, HIPAA, ISO 27001, and SOC 2, require or strongly recommend periodic penetration testing as part of an organization's security assurance activities. These tests help demonstrate due diligence, support audit readiness, and provide documented evidence that proactive steps are being taken to identify and address security risks. In regulated industries such as finance, healthcare, and critical infrastructure, penetration testing is often seen not just as a best practice but as a necessary element of operational integrity.

The success of a penetration test depends heavily on the skill and experience of the testing team. Organizations must carefully select qualified professionals who understand not only the technical aspects of security but also the specific business context of the systems they are testing. Effective testers communicate clearly, document their findings thoroughly, and provide actionable recommendations that align with the organization's risk management objectives. Post-engagement debriefings or workshops are often held to walk through the results, clarify technical details, and prioritize remediation steps. These sessions foster collaboration between security, development, and operations teams and help translate testing outcomes into meaningful improvements.

It is important to recognize that penetration testing is not a replacement for other security activities but a complement to them. While it provides depth and context, it cannot cover every device, user, or application in the organization. Automated scanning, patch management, security monitoring, and user awareness training must all work in concert with penetration testing to provide comprehensive protection. A mature vulnerability management program integrates the results of penetration tests with other data sources, such as configuration audits, threat intelligence, and incident reports, to develop a holistic view of the organization's risk landscape.

By including penetration testing as a core element of the vulnerability management strategy, organizations gain valuable insights into how their systems can be attacked and what the real consequences of those attacks would be. These insights help drive better decisions, strengthen defenses, and improve response capabilities. In a world where threats are constantly evolving and attackers adapt rapidly, the human insight provided by skilled penetration testers offers a level of depth, creativity, and contextual understanding that cannot be matched by automation alone. Penetration testing ultimately enhances the organization's ability to detect, withstand, and recover from security threats, contributing significantly to long-term resilience and trust.

Red Team vs Blue Team in Vulnerability Context

The dynamic between red teams and blue teams plays a vital role in the broader framework of vulnerability management, offering a real-time, adversarial simulation that pushes an organization to confront the practical effectiveness of its security controls, response protocols, and overall preparedness. This simulated conflict mirrors real-world attack and defense scenarios, where red teams assume the role of attackers aiming to exploit vulnerabilities, and blue teams act as defenders responsible for identifying, containing, and mitigating threats. By framing vulnerability management within this adversarial context, organizations gain critical insight into how well their systems, people, and processes function under pressure.

Red team exercises go beyond conventional penetration testing by incorporating stealth, persistence, and a focus on objectives rather than simply identifying weaknesses. A red team is tasked with mimicking the tactics, techniques, and procedures of real-world threat actors, including nation-state groups, cybercriminals, and insider threats. This team may use social engineering, spear-phishing, physical intrusion, and exploitation of zero-day vulnerabilities to gain initial access and escalate privileges. Their goal is not merely to find flaws but to demonstrate how those flaws can be chained together to compromise critical assets, exfiltrate data, or cause operational disruption. Red team operations are designed to be as realistic as possible, often operating without the knowledge of the blue team to simulate a genuine attack scenario.

Blue teams, on the other hand, are responsible for maintaining and defending the organization's networks, endpoints, applications, and data. Their role in the red versus blue exercise is to detect and respond to red team activities in real time, using their existing tools, procedures, and expertise. This includes monitoring logs, analyzing alerts, conducting forensic investigations, and deploying countermeasures to isolate compromised systems. Blue teams must correlate disparate pieces of information to identify the attack chain, understand the red team's movements, and take effective action. These exercises test the effectiveness of detection technologies such as intrusion detection systems, SIEM platforms, and endpoint detection and response tools, while also evaluating the human element—how quickly and accurately the defenders respond to unfolding threats.

In the context of vulnerability management, the interaction between red and blue teams highlights not just which vulnerabilities exist, but how exploitable they are in a real-world scenario. A vulnerability that appears severe on paper may prove difficult to exploit in practice due to environmental factors or layered defenses. Conversely, a medium-severity flaw may be the weak link that allows an attacker to bypass critical controls. Red team exercises bring this nuance into sharp focus, enabling organizations to reassess their prioritization models based on actual exploitation potential rather than theoretical risk alone. Blue teams benefit by refining their detection capabilities and developing playbooks to recognize and contain similar tactics in future incidents.

The lessons learned from red and blue team engagements feed directly into continuous improvement. After the exercise, a debrief session—often referred to as a purple team session—brings both sides together to share observations, compare notes, and discuss what worked, what failed, and what could be improved. This collaborative phase is where the real value is unlocked. Red teams explain how they bypassed defenses, what vulnerabilities they exploited, and how they maintained persistence. Blue teams discuss their detection and response timeline, the challenges they encountered, and any false positives or missed signals. This mutual exchange leads to actionable recommendations, including hardening configurations, tuning detection rules, improving alert triage, and refining incident response procedures.

Red versus blue team exercises also test the broader ecosystem of the organization. Beyond technical controls, they evaluate policies, communication channels, and decision-making structures. For example, how quickly can the security team escalate an issue to leadership? Are incident response roles clearly defined? Does the organization have the capability to isolate affected systems without causing unnecessary disruption? The red team may deliberately target systems that are critical to operations or probe weaknesses in business processes, such as vendor access or remote work infrastructure. The blue team must be prepared not only to detect and respond to these threats but also to manage the incident within the constraints of organizational realities and business continuity requirements.

Another important aspect of red and blue team exercises is their impact on security culture. These simulations provide a tangible and engaging way to demonstrate the importance of security, highlight the consequences of poor practices, and reinforce the need for vigilance. For blue teams, the experience is a hands-on opportunity to hone skills, build confidence, and validate their capabilities. For red teams, it is a chance to think creatively, simulate realistic threats, and challenge assumptions. The interaction fosters mutual respect and breaks down adversarial silos, leading to better collaboration and shared responsibility for securing the organization.

Over time, organizations may evolve their approach to include persistent red team operations and formalize blue team readiness programs. These ongoing efforts transform one-time assessments into continuous evaluation and learning cycles. Automation and threat intelligence can be layered into blue team activities to accelerate detection and response, while red teams can leverage emerging attack vectors to ensure their tactics remain current. By maintaining this adversarial loop, organizations create a living laboratory for cybersecurity, one that adapts to new technologies, threat actors, and organizational changes.

Integrating red and blue team dynamics into vulnerability management also bridges gaps between tactical findings and strategic decisions. It provides security leaders with evidence-based insights that go beyond compliance checklists or scanner reports. Executives can see firsthand how vulnerabilities translate into risk, how security investments perform under pressure, and where improvements are most urgently needed. This perspective supports more informed budgeting, prioritization, and policy development, aligning security initiatives with business objectives.

Ultimately, the red team versus blue team approach in the context of vulnerability management represents a shift from passive defense to active, intelligence-driven security. It embraces complexity, recognizes that breaches are inevitable, and focuses on reducing the time to detect and respond. By simulating the adversary and testing defenders under realistic conditions, organizations gain clarity on their strengths and weaknesses. They move beyond theoretical assessments to practical resilience, building not just a secure infrastructure but a capable, adaptive security operation prepared to meet the evolving threat landscape.

Compliance Requirements and Regulations

Compliance requirements and regulations are central to modern cybersecurity practices, including vulnerability management. Organizations across all industries must navigate a complex landscape of legal obligations, industry standards, and contractual commitments that govern how they protect data, secure systems, and respond to threats. These regulations are designed to safeguard consumers, preserve the integrity of critical infrastructure, and establish accountability for how organizations handle digital risk. Meeting compliance requirements is not simply a matter of checking boxes; it is a structured approach to embedding security controls that ensure vulnerabilities are identified, prioritized, and remediated in a timely and verifiable manner. Failing to comply can result in legal penalties, reputational damage, financial loss, and even operational shutdowns in regulated industries.

One of the foundational compliance standards is the Payment Card Industry Data Security Standard, commonly known as PCI DSS. This standard applies to any organization that stores, processes, or transmits credit card data. Among its many requirements, PCI DSS mandates that organizations implement a formal vulnerability management program. This includes running internal and external vulnerability scans on a regular basis, applying security patches within specific timeframes, and conducting penetration tests at least annually or after major changes. Non-compliance with PCI DSS can result in substantial fines, increased transaction fees, and even the loss of the ability to process card payments. The enforcement of vulnerability management in PCI DSS underscores how compliance frameworks view the rapid remediation of known flaws as critical to reducing the risk of data breaches.

In the healthcare sector, the Health Insurance Portability and Accountability Act, or HIPAA, sets forth standards for safeguarding protected health information. HIPAA's Security Rule requires covered entities and their business associates to implement administrative, physical, and technical safeguards, including risk assessment and management practices. While HIPAA does not prescribe specific tools or technologies, it does expect organizations to regularly assess vulnerabilities, manage risks, and ensure the confidentiality, integrity, and availability of electronic health information. This includes patching systems, mitigating known threats, and documenting security incidents and responses. Compliance with HIPAA is overseen by the U.S. Department of Health and Human Services, which has the authority to issue significant fines for violations, especially when breaches are caused by unaddressed vulnerabilities that could have been prevented.

Another major regulation that drives vulnerability management practices is the General Data Protection Regulation, or GDPR. Enforced across the European Union and applying to any organization that handles personal data of EU residents, GDPR places a strong emphasis on accountability and data protection by design and by default. Article 32 of GDPR requires organizations to implement appropriate technical and organizational measures to ensure a level of security appropriate to the risk. This includes the ability to detect, respond to, and recover from data breaches. Regular testing, assessment, and evaluation of security measures are explicitly required, making vulnerability management a critical component of GDPR compliance. Regulatory authorities under GDPR can impose fines of up to four percent of an organization's annual global turnover for serious violations, providing a strong incentive for maintaining effective and demonstrable security controls.

In the financial sector, regulations such as the Sarbanes-Oxley Act, the Gramm-Leach-Bliley Act, and the Federal Financial Institutions Examination Council (FFIEC) guidelines require firms to implement and document robust internal controls, including those related to IT systems and information security. These regulations aim to ensure the reliability of financial reporting, protect consumer data, and maintain confidence in the financial system. Vulnerability management supports these goals by ensuring that systems are protected from known threats and that incidents can be prevented, detected, and addressed in a timely manner. Documentation, audit trails, and regular assessments are essential to proving compliance during inspections or investigations.

The energy sector is governed by the North American Electric Reliability Corporation Critical Infrastructure Protection standards, or NERC CIP. These standards apply to organizations responsible for the operation of the bulk electric system and include detailed requirements for identifying, classifying, and protecting critical cyber assets. Vulnerability assessments, patch management, and incident response are core components of NERC CIP compliance. The standards are prescriptive and require strict documentation and adherence to defined timelines for mitigating known vulnerabilities. Because energy infrastructure is considered part of national security, non-compliance with NERC CIP can result in not only fines but also reputational scrutiny and operational mandates.

Beyond industry-specific regulations, many organizations are subject to broader compliance frameworks and certifications such as ISO/IEC 27001, SOC 2, and the Cybersecurity Maturity Model Certification. These frameworks provide structured guidelines for establishing, implementing, maintaining, and improving information security management systems. While voluntary in some cases, they are often required by business partners, government contracts, or market expectations. These standards emphasize continuous improvement, risk-based decision-making, and the integration of security into all aspects of business operations. Vulnerability management plays a key role by providing the mechanisms for identifying and controlling technical weaknesses that could undermine security objectives.

The rise of cloud computing has introduced new compliance considerations, as organizations must extend their responsibility for security to include third-party service providers. Regulations such as the Cloud Security Alliance's Cloud Controls Matrix and the shared responsibility models of major cloud platforms require customers to ensure that vulnerabilities in cloud-hosted systems are addressed even if the infrastructure is managed by the provider. Misconfigurations, unpatched systems, and weak access controls in cloud environments are still the customer's responsibility and can lead to compliance failures if not managed properly. This has led to the development of cloud-specific compliance tools and automation platforms that help organizations maintain visibility and control over their cloud security posture.

One of the challenges of managing compliance across multiple regulations is the overlap and variation between frameworks. Organizations must often map requirements from different standards and implement controls that satisfy multiple obligations simultaneously. Centralizing vulnerability data, maintaining accurate asset inventories, automating patch management, and generating standardized reports are essential capabilities that support this multi-regulatory environment. Governance, risk, and compliance platforms can help streamline these efforts by consolidating information, aligning processes, and providing a unified view of compliance status across the organization.

Ultimately, compliance requirements and regulations serve as both a baseline and a catalyst for effective vulnerability management. They define the minimum expectations for protecting systems and data, but they also push organizations to adopt best practices, improve accountability, and foster a culture of security. Rather than being viewed as a burden, compliance should be understood as an opportunity to build trust with customers, partners, and regulators. Organizations that embrace compliance as part of their operational DNA are better positioned to respond to evolving threats, maintain resilience, and thrive in a digital economy where security and trust are essential.

Mapping Vulnerabilities to Frameworks (e.g., NIST, ISO)

Mapping vulnerabilities to established security frameworks such as the National Institute of Standards and Technology (NIST) and the International Organization for Standardization (ISO) provides organizations with a structured method for aligning their vulnerability management efforts with recognized best practices. These frameworks are designed to provide strategic guidance, technical standards, and operational controls to ensure organizations can manage information security risks in a consistent and repeatable manner. When vulnerabilities are discovered in systems, applications, or processes, aligning their remediation to framework requirements ensures that actions taken are not only reactive but strategically sound and auditable. This mapping supports regulatory compliance, risk management, and the continuous improvement of security programs.

The NIST Cybersecurity Framework (CSF) offers a comprehensive model that includes five core functions: Identify, Protect, Detect, Respond, and Recover. Each of these functions is divided into categories and subcategories that outline specific security outcomes. Vulnerability management is primarily addressed in the Identify and Protect functions but has implications across all five. For example, within the Identify function, asset management and risk assessments help organizations understand what needs to be protected and which vulnerabilities present the highest risk. Under the Protect function, vulnerability management is directly referenced through subcategories such as PR.IP-12, which focuses on the management of vulnerabilities within organizational assets. Mapping discovered vulnerabilities to these categories ensures that remediation efforts are documented and aligned with broader security goals.

Similarly, the NIST Special Publication 800-53 provides a catalog of security and privacy controls for federal information systems, which is often adopted by private-sector organizations as well. Within this publication, the System and Communications Protection (SC) and Risk Assessment (RA) control families are particularly relevant to vulnerability management. Controls such as RA-5, which requires organizations to scan for vulnerabilities and remediate them, provide a clear directive that can be directly mapped to vulnerability assessment activities. By tagging each vulnerability finding with the relevant NIST control, security teams create traceability that supports audits, risk assessments, and executive reporting. This mapping also allows for automated compliance validation when using governance, risk, and compliance platforms that support control-based dashboards.

The ISO/IEC 27001 standard, part of the ISO 27000 family, offers a globally recognized framework for establishing, implementing, maintaining, and continuously improving an information security management system (ISMS). In the context of vulnerability management, ISO 27001 requires organizations to apply controls listed in Annex A, specifically control A.12.6.1, which mandates the timely response to technical vulnerabilities. This includes identifying, assessing, and taking appropriate measures to mitigate vulnerabilities in a timely manner. Mapping discovered vulnerabilities to this control allows organizations to demonstrate their adherence to the ISO standard and to ensure their ISMS is both operational and effective. Furthermore, ISO's emphasis on risk-based decision-making reinforces the need to prioritize vulnerabilities based on business impact, exploitability, and threat intelligence, rather than relying solely on technical severity.

Beyond NIST and ISO, other frameworks such as the Center for Internet Security (CIS) Controls and COBIT also support the mapping of vulnerability management activities. The CIS Controls, particularly Control 7 on continuous vulnerability management, provide prescriptive, actionable steps for identifying and remediating weaknesses. These include automated scanning, patch management, and the use of threat intelligence to guide prioritization. Mapping vulnerabilities to these controls helps organizations follow a prioritized path toward improving their security posture. The CIS Controls are also frequently used in combination with NIST CSF to create tailored, industry-specific implementations of security best practices.

Mapping vulnerabilities to frameworks also facilitates communication between technical teams and executive stakeholders. Security leaders often struggle to translate raw vulnerability data into language that aligns with business objectives and governance structures. By framing vulnerabilities in terms of compliance with NIST, ISO, or CIS controls, security professionals can provide context that resonates with boards of directors, risk committees, and compliance officers. This approach enables more informed decision-making about resource allocation, risk acceptance, and investment in security technologies. For example, presenting a vulnerability as a gap in NIST CSF's PR.IP-12 control provides a more strategic narrative than simply listing a CVSS score or technical description.

Automation plays an increasing role in vulnerability-to-framework mapping. Modern vulnerability management platforms are capable of tagging each discovered vulnerability with relevant framework controls using pre-built libraries and rule sets. These platforms integrate with asset inventories, ticketing systems, and SIEM tools to create a closed-loop process in which vulnerabilities are identified, assigned, remediated, and documented in accordance with defined controls. This automation not only increases operational efficiency but also provides real-time insight into compliance status. Dashboards can show how many vulnerabilities are associated with each framework control, how many are open or overdue, and which assets pose the highest risk. These insights drive continuous improvement by highlighting areas of weakness and tracking progress over time.

It is also important to consider the flexibility that framework mapping provides in response to emerging threats and changing environments. As new vulnerabilities emerge and attack techniques evolve, frameworks such as NIST and ISO can be updated or interpreted to accommodate new realities. Security teams can adjust their mapping strategies to reflect new control objectives, threat landscapes, or business requirements. This adaptability ensures that vulnerability management remains aligned with both industry standards and organizational needs. It also supports risk-based approaches that account for the context in which vulnerabilities exist, including exposure, exploit availability, and asset value.

Framework mapping is not only useful during active vulnerability remediation but also plays a crucial role in retrospective analysis and audits. During compliance audits, security teams must demonstrate how they detected vulnerabilities, what actions were taken to address them, and how those actions align with relevant controls. By maintaining documentation and evidence that links vulnerability data to framework requirements, organizations streamline audit preparation and reduce the risk of penalties or non-compliance findings. This documentation is also valuable for internal audits, risk assessments, and executive reporting, as it provides a comprehensive view of the organization's ability to manage cyber risk.

Incorporating framework-based mapping into vulnerability management is ultimately about maturity and alignment. It reflects an organization's commitment to disciplined, transparent, and strategic security practices. Rather than treating each vulnerability as an isolated issue, this approach embeds vulnerabilities within a broader context of governance and continuous improvement. It allows organizations to demonstrate due diligence, meet regulatory requirements, and build a resilient security posture that evolves with the threat landscape. By grounding their efforts in widely respected frameworks such as NIST and ISO, organizations create a common language for cybersecurity that bridges technical operations and business oversight, ensuring that vulnerability management becomes a core function of both security and governance.

Reporting and Metrics for Executives

Reporting and metrics for executives in the context of vulnerability management are essential to translate complex technical data into meaningful, actionable insights that support business decisions. Executives are responsible for aligning cybersecurity strategies with organizational goals, ensuring regulatory compliance, and maintaining the trust of stakeholders. They are not typically interested in the raw details of individual vulnerabilities or the intricacies of scanning tools. Instead, they require high-level visibility into how well the organization is managing risk, where weaknesses exist, how those weaknesses are being addressed, and what the broader implications are for operations, reputation, and financial performance. Effective reporting bridges the gap between technical security operations and strategic business leadership.

A well-designed executive report on vulnerability management focuses on summarizing key performance indicators that reflect the organization's security posture over time. These indicators include the total number of vulnerabilities discovered, the number of critical or high-severity vulnerabilities, the average time to remediation, and the percentage of vulnerabilities resolved within defined service level agreements. These core metrics help executives understand whether the organization is improving, stagnating, or falling behind in its ability to manage cyber risk. When presented in a clear and visually digestible format, such as dashboards, charts, and trend lines, these metrics provide a concise snapshot of risk exposure and remediation efforts without requiring technical interpretation.

Executives are particularly concerned with risk to the business. Therefore, reporting should go beyond the count of vulnerabilities to highlight risk-based prioritization. Not every vulnerability poses the same level of threat, and a report that treats all issues equally fails to capture their true impact. For instance, a vulnerability affecting a high-value asset, such as a database containing customer information, is far more significant than a similar vulnerability on a test system with no sensitive data. Risk-based metrics might include the number of vulnerabilities on mission-critical systems, vulnerabilities with known exploits in the wild, or those that could lead to regulatory non-compliance. Incorporating asset value and exploitability into the reporting structure allows executives to make informed decisions about resource allocation, remediation timelines, and risk acceptance.

Another important aspect of executive reporting is benchmarking. Organizations benefit from comparing their current vulnerability management performance against historical data, industry standards, or peers in the same sector. Trends over time, such as improvements in remediation speed or reductions in high-risk exposure, demonstrate progress and maturity. Conversely, negative trends highlight areas requiring immediate attention or investment. Benchmarking can also support strategic planning by identifying patterns and predicting future risk scenarios. For example, if vulnerabilities in third-party components are consistently responsible for a large portion of the organization's risk, executives might prioritize initiatives to improve software supply chain security or vendor management practices.

Metrics must also address compliance requirements. Many executives are accountable for ensuring that their organizations meet the standards set by regulatory bodies, contractual obligations, or internal governance frameworks. Reporting should include coverage metrics that show how well the organization is meeting defined security controls. Examples include the percentage of systems scanned within a given timeframe, the percentage of critical vulnerabilities remediated within SLA, and compliance with framework-specific controls such as those from NIST, ISO, or CIS. These compliance metrics not only support audits and regulatory submissions but also provide assurance to boards and stakeholders that the organization is taking appropriate steps to mitigate cybersecurity risks.

Effective executive reporting also involves storytelling. Raw metrics become powerful when accompanied by narrative explanations that contextualize the data. Reports should explain why certain metrics matter, what actions were taken in response to previous findings, and what strategic initiatives are underway to improve security posture. For instance, a spike in vulnerabilities might be attributed to a recent acquisition or system upgrade, and the report should outline how that risk is being addressed. Similarly, a sustained reduction in critical vulnerabilities might be the result of a successful patch automation initiative, which can be highlighted as a positive return on investment. These narratives allow executives to see cybersecurity not just as a cost center, but as a business enabler.

Audience segmentation is another key principle in reporting. Not all executives require the same level of detail. A chief financial officer might focus on the financial implications of unresolved vulnerabilities, such as the cost of potential breaches or investments required for remediation. A chief operating officer may want to understand the impact of vulnerabilities on operational continuity or system availability. A board member might be most interested in how cybersecurity risks relate to reputational harm or regulatory exposure. Tailoring reports to the specific concerns and responsibilities of each executive ensures that the information is relevant, digestible, and actionable.

To maintain consistency and transparency, vulnerability management reports should follow a regular cadence, whether monthly, quarterly, or aligned with board meetings. This allows for the development of a baseline and the ability to detect trends over time. Reports should be archived and referenced in future assessments to measure progress and demonstrate accountability. In times of incident response or heightened scrutiny, having a historical record of how vulnerabilities have been managed builds trust and credibility with internal and external stakeholders.

Technology plays a supporting role in streamlining reporting. Integrated dashboards, data visualization platforms, and security information and event management systems can automate much of the data collection and presentation process. These tools should be configured to extract data from vulnerability scanners, asset management systems, patch management tools, and incident response platforms to create a unified view of vulnerability management. Automation reduces the manual effort required to compile reports and increases the accuracy and timeliness of information. However, the human element remains vital in interpreting the data, providing context, and aligning security efforts with business strategy.

Ultimately, reporting and metrics for executives should drive informed decision-making. They should enable leadership to assess whether the organization is effectively reducing risk, investing in the right areas, and responding to emerging threats in a timely and coordinated manner. By presenting vulnerability data in a structured, contextualized, and business-oriented format, security leaders can foster meaningful engagement with executives, secure the resources needed to improve defenses, and support a culture of accountability and continuous improvement across the organization. The goal is not merely to report numbers but to inspire action, guide strategy, and build resilience in an increasingly complex and hostile digital environment.

Building a Vulnerability Management Policy

Building a vulnerability management policy is a fundamental step toward establishing a structured and sustainable approach to identifying, assessing, prioritizing, remediating, and tracking vulnerabilities within an organization's systems and infrastructure. A well-crafted policy ensures that vulnerability management efforts are aligned with business objectives, regulatory requirements, and risk tolerance levels. It creates accountability across departments and provides the foundation for a repeatable and measurable process. As cyber threats continue to evolve in complexity and volume, organizations must have a documented framework that defines how vulnerabilities will be managed throughout their lifecycle. This policy not only standardizes expectations but also promotes organizational awareness and collaboration in maintaining a secure environment.

The process of building a vulnerability management policy begins with defining its purpose and scope. The policy must articulate the organization's commitment to proactive vulnerability management and explain why such a program is essential to reducing risk. The scope should clearly state which systems, assets, networks, applications, and business processes are covered. This includes both internally managed and third-party components, as well as systems that support critical operations, contain sensitive data, or are exposed to public networks. By establishing a comprehensive scope, the policy ensures that no critical systems are excluded from oversight due to ambiguity or oversight.

Roles and responsibilities are at the core of an effective vulnerability management policy. The policy must identify which teams and individuals are responsible for vulnerability scanning, assessment, remediation, and verification. This typically involves collaboration between information security, IT operations, application development, asset owners, and executive leadership. The security team may lead vulnerability identification and risk analysis, while IT operations apply patches and configuration changes. Asset owners provide business context, helping to assess the importance of the affected systems and the potential impact of a vulnerability. Clear assignment of responsibilities ensures accountability and avoids delays in remediation due to confusion over ownership.

Another essential component of the policy is the frequency of vulnerability assessments. The organization must define how often vulnerability scans will be conducted, what types of scans will be performed, and under what conditions. Regular scanning may include weekly or monthly assessments for internal systems, daily scans for internet-facing assets, and ad hoc scans following significant changes such as software deployments or infrastructure upgrades. The policy should also outline how emergency scans are triggered in response to high-profile vulnerabilities or incidents. These procedures help maintain consistent visibility into the organization's risk posture and ensure that vulnerabilities are identified as early as possible.

Once vulnerabilities are discovered, the policy must define how they are assessed and prioritized. Not all vulnerabilities represent equal risk, and a risk-based approach is essential to effective management. The policy should describe how severity is determined, which may include factors such as CVSS scores, exploit availability, asset criticality, data sensitivity, and exposure. The organization may adopt a tiered model that defines priority levels based on the potential impact of exploitation. For example, a critical vulnerability on a public-facing server hosting customer data may be assigned the highest priority, while a medium vulnerability on a non-critical internal system receives lower urgency. Establishing these criteria in the policy ensures consistent and objective prioritization across teams.

Timeframes for remediation are another key element. The policy must define service level objectives for addressing vulnerabilities based on their priority. For instance, critical vulnerabilities may be required to be remediated within 24 to 72 hours, while lower-priority issues may have a 30-day or 60-day window. These timeframes set expectations, drive accountability, and allow performance to be measured against defined benchmarks. The policy should also provide guidance on exceptions, such as when remediation is delayed due to technical constraints, business dependencies, or the need for additional testing. In such cases, compensating controls must be considered and documented to mitigate the risk until full remediation can be completed.

The verification of remediation efforts is a crucial step in closing the vulnerability management loop. The policy should define how remediation actions are validated, such as through rescanning, configuration audits, or manual verification. Ensuring that vulnerabilities are actually resolved, rather than merely assumed to be addressed, strengthens the integrity of the process. The policy may also include procedures for tracking the effectiveness of remediation efforts over time, such as measuring how often vulnerabilities reappear or whether recurring issues point to deeper problems in development or operations.

Reporting and communication protocols are vital for transparency and continuous improvement. The policy should specify how vulnerability data will be reported, to whom, and how frequently. Reports may include summary statistics for executives, detailed remediation metrics for technical teams, and compliance dashboards for audit and risk management functions. Communication channels must also be established for coordinating across departments, escalating issues, and informing stakeholders of significant vulnerabilities or delays. Timely and accurate communication ensures that all parties are aligned and that vulnerabilities are not ignored due to a lack of awareness.

Integration with other security and IT processes is another important consideration. The vulnerability management policy should align with incident response, change management, configuration management, and patch management policies. This alignment ensures that vulnerability remediation is performed in a controlled and traceable manner, minimizes the risk of introducing new problems during fixes, and supports compliance with internal controls and regulatory standards. For example, a change request may be required before applying a patch in a production environment, and that change must be tracked and approved according to established procedures.

Training and awareness are also addressed in a comprehensive vulnerability management policy. Employees and contractors who interact with systems must understand their role in maintaining security. This may include awareness of phishing attacks, best practices for system configuration, or procedures for reporting suspicious activity. Developers should be trained in secure coding practices, while system administrators must understand the tools and techniques used for identifying and resolving vulnerabilities. Ongoing education helps embed security into the organization's culture and ensures that personnel have the knowledge needed to execute the policy effectively.

Finally, the policy must define how it will be reviewed, updated, and enforced. Vulnerability management is a dynamic discipline, and the policy must evolve with changes in technology, threat landscapes, organizational structure, and regulatory requirements. A regular review cycle, such as annually or after significant incidents, helps keep the policy relevant and effective. Enforcement mechanisms, such as audits, key performance indicators, and disciplinary measures, provide the accountability needed to ensure compliance. By treating the vulnerability management policy as a living document that reflects the organization's strategic priorities, security teams can maintain a proactive stance in managing risk and protecting critical assets.

Creating Repeatable Processes

Creating repeatable processes in vulnerability management is essential to transforming ad hoc, reactive security practices into scalable, efficient, and resilient operations. As organizations grow in size and complexity, the number of systems, applications, users, and potential attack vectors multiplies. Without a consistent and repeatable approach to identifying, assessing, and remediating vulnerabilities, efforts become fragmented and unreliable. Repeatable processes serve as the foundation for maturity in any security program, enabling consistent results, accelerating response times, and ensuring accountability across teams. They allow organizations to operate in a state of continuous vigilance, where known weaknesses are addressed methodically and emerging threats are handled swiftly and with precision.

The first step in building repeatable processes is standardizing how vulnerabilities are discovered. This means implementing automated scanning solutions that run on a fixed schedule and cover all relevant assets, including servers, workstations, cloud environments, containers, and network devices. These scans should follow clearly defined parameters for what is to be assessed, how often the scans occur, and what tools are used. Automating this stage eliminates the risk of missing scans due to human error and ensures that all systems are consistently evaluated. Moreover, defining scanning frequency based on asset criticality ensures that higher-risk systems receive more frequent scrutiny, while lower-priority systems are scanned according to acceptable risk thresholds.

Once vulnerabilities are identified, the next repeatable process involves classification and prioritization. This is where a structured framework is vital. Organizations should establish clear criteria for assigning severity to vulnerabilities, such as using CVSS scores in combination with asset criticality, network exposure, business value, and exploit availability. This risk-based approach allows security teams to focus on the vulnerabilities that matter most and prevents time from being wasted on low-risk issues. To make the process repeatable, these criteria must be codified in policy and consistently applied by all team members. Automation can assist here as well, with vulnerability management platforms assigning risk scores and filtering results based on predefined thresholds.

Another key process that must be repeatable is the assignment of ownership for remediation. Each identified vulnerability must be traced to a responsible party, whether that be a system administrator, a developer, or a third-party vendor. Roles and responsibilities should be well-documented so that when a vulnerability appears on a specific asset, there is no confusion over who is responsible for fixing it. The process of assigning and tracking remediation tasks should be managed through a centralized ticketing system or workflow platform, ensuring that issues are not lost or delayed. Repeatable workflows include automated ticket creation, deadline setting based on severity, and escalation paths for overdue remediation.

Patching and mitigation workflows represent another area where repeatability is essential. Organizations must define and document the exact steps for applying updates, rolling out patches, conducting pre-deployment testing, and validating the effectiveness of the fix. This applies to operating systems, third-party applications, firmware, and configurations. The process should be coordinated with change management procedures to avoid disrupting operations. Repeatable patch management ensures that similar vulnerabilities are addressed consistently across all instances, regardless of who is performing the remediation. By integrating patching into the CI/CD pipeline for development environments and scheduling regular maintenance windows for production systems, organizations can systematically reduce their attack surface.

Verification processes confirm that remediation efforts are successful and must be just as consistent. Rescanning assets after remediation, validating that vulnerabilities no longer appear, and checking that system functionality has not been impacted are critical steps in closing the loop. A repeatable verification process includes documenting the remediation action, scheduling rescans automatically, and updating tickets with verification results. This ensures that vulnerabilities are not only addressed but confirmed as resolved, maintaining the integrity of the vulnerability management program and preparing the organization for audits and compliance assessments.

Metrics and reporting play an integral role in sustaining repeatable processes. By collecting and analyzing data on the number of vulnerabilities discovered, the average time to remediation, compliance with service level objectives, and the rate of recurring issues, security teams can identify gaps in the process and drive continuous improvement. Metrics should be reported regularly to both technical and executive audiences, highlighting successes, identifying bottlenecks, and providing a roadmap for enhancing capabilities. These reports should be generated using standardized templates and updated on a consistent schedule, allowing stakeholders to track progress and make informed decisions.

Training and knowledge sharing are also essential components of a repeatable process framework. Team members must be trained on how to use scanning tools, interpret results, prioritize findings, and execute remediation tasks in accordance with established procedures. When new tools are introduced or existing workflows are updated, documentation and training materials must be revised and redistributed. A repeatable onboarding process for new security team members ensures that all staff are aligned with the organization's vulnerability management methodology from day one. Knowledge bases, playbooks, and internal wikis can serve as central repositories for process documentation, enabling fast reference and consistency in execution.

Communication protocols help ensure that repeatable processes function smoothly across departments. Security cannot operate in isolation, and the success of vulnerability management depends on timely and effective collaboration between IT, development, compliance, and business units. A repeatable communication process includes structured updates, escalation procedures, feedback loops, and incident coordination plans. Standard meeting cadences, such as weekly syncs or monthly reviews, provide opportunities to align on priorities, discuss challenges, and refine processes. Maintaining a consistent rhythm of communication ensures that vulnerability management efforts remain synchronized with broader organizational goals.

The ability to scale vulnerability management depends entirely on the repeatability of its processes. As the number of assets increases, and as threats become more sophisticated, manual and inconsistent methods become unmanageable. Repeatable processes allow for automation, delegation, and scalability. They also support regulatory compliance by providing a clear, auditable trail of activity and evidence of due diligence. Most importantly, they embed security into the organization's culture, transforming it from a reactive discipline into a proactive, strategic function that enables innovation while protecting assets.

Building these processes requires an upfront investment of time, planning, and resources, but the payoff is significant. A mature, repeatable vulnerability management program improves security outcomes, reduces risk exposure, accelerates incident response, and supports business continuity. It provides a foundation for resilience in a threat landscape that continues to evolve and ensures that the organization is prepared not just for the vulnerabilities it knows about, but also for the ones that have yet to be discovered.

Automation in Vulnerability Management

Automation in vulnerability management is transforming how organizations handle the growing complexity, scale, and speed of modern cyber threats. As networks expand, cloud environments proliferate, and software becomes increasingly modular and decentralized, the volume of potential vulnerabilities rises exponentially. Manually managing the lifecycle of these vulnerabilities—from detection to remediation and verification—is no longer feasible in large or even medium-sized environments. Automation addresses this challenge by enabling organizations to respond to vulnerabilities with speed, consistency, and accuracy. It eliminates human error, streamlines workflows, and ensures that security policies are applied uniformly across a dynamic and evolving infrastructure.

At the core of automation in vulnerability management is the integration of scanning tools that operate on a scheduled basis or in real-time, continuously scanning systems for known vulnerabilities. These tools interface directly with endpoints, cloud resources, web applications, and container environments to identify software flaws, configuration weaknesses, and missing patches. The automation of this discovery process allows for immediate identification of risks as new vulnerabilities are disclosed or as assets change. Automated scanning also ensures that the organization maintains complete and up-to-date visibility into its attack surface, including newly added devices or systems that might otherwise be overlooked.

Once vulnerabilities are detected, automation plays a vital role in prioritization. Instead of manually sorting through long lists of findings, automated tools correlate vulnerability data with threat intelligence feeds, asset criticality scores, and exploit availability databases. This allows the system to generate contextual risk scores that rank vulnerabilities based on their real-world impact. For instance, a critical vulnerability in a publicly exposed database server with active exploit code would be prioritized higher than a similar flaw on an isolated test machine. Automated risk scoring reduces the noise in vulnerability reports and enables security teams to focus on the most pressing threats without wasting time on low-risk issues.

Automation continues into the next phase of the vulnerability lifecycle: assignment and remediation. Integration with IT service management platforms allows vulnerabilities to be automatically converted into remediation tickets. These tickets are assigned to the appropriate asset owners or system administrators based on predefined rules and roles. For example, a vulnerability found on a Linux server might be routed to the infrastructure team, while a flaw in a custom application might go to the development team. Automated ticket generation includes all necessary details such as vulnerability description, affected asset, recommended fix, and deadline based on service level objectives. This process minimizes delays, eliminates guesswork, and creates a clear path for remediation activities.

In environments where patching can be automated, such as cloud infrastructure or managed endpoints, the entire remediation process can be executed without human intervention. Security orchestration platforms can deploy patches, restart services, or adjust configurations in response to vulnerabilities identified during scans. This is especially effective for routine or low-risk fixes that do not require manual validation. For more critical systems, automation can facilitate the remediation process by preparing patches, alerting stakeholders, and scheduling updates during maintenance windows, ensuring that security improvements are made swiftly while maintaining operational stability.

Automation also enhances the verification process. After remediation, systems can be automatically rescanned to confirm that vulnerabilities have been resolved. If a fix is unsuccessful or if a patch fails to apply, the system can reopen the ticket, escalate the issue, or trigger an alternative remediation workflow. Automated verification eliminates the risk of assuming that a vulnerability has been fixed simply because a task was marked complete. It provides measurable assurance that the remediation was effective and supports compliance efforts by maintaining an auditable record of each remediation cycle.

In addition to operational efficiency, automation improves the quality and consistency of reporting. Security teams can use automated tools to generate dashboards and metrics that reflect the current state of vulnerability exposure across the organization. These reports can be customized for different audiences, from technical staff to executive leadership. Automation ensures that reports are generated on time, use consistent data sources, and reflect the most recent scan results and remediation statuses. It also enables real-time reporting, which is critical during audits, incident investigations, or periods of heightened threat activity. Continuous visibility into vulnerability trends helps organizations track progress, identify bottlenecks, and allocate resources more effectively.

Another significant benefit of automation in vulnerability management is its ability to scale. As organizations grow, the number of assets to monitor and secure increases dramatically. Manual processes simply cannot keep up with the velocity of change in modern IT environments. Automation allows security programs to scale proportionally, handling thousands or even millions of vulnerability events without compromising on speed or accuracy. This scalability is especially important in cloud-native and hybrid environments where infrastructure is ephemeral, workloads move dynamically, and traditional perimeter-based defenses are no longer sufficient. Automated tools adapt to this new reality by continuously discovering, assessing, and responding to vulnerabilities wherever they appear.

Security teams can also leverage automation to simulate attacks and test the effectiveness of their vulnerability management program. By integrating automated penetration testing or breach and attack simulation tools, organizations can validate whether remediated vulnerabilities truly mitigate the threat or whether additional controls are needed. These simulations run autonomously and mimic attacker behavior, helping teams refine their detection and response capabilities in a safe, controlled environment. When combined with automated vulnerability management, these tools create a feedback loop that strengthens the entire security ecosystem.

Automation does not eliminate the need for human oversight. Rather, it elevates the role of security professionals by freeing them from repetitive tasks and enabling them to focus on higher-level strategic work. Analysts can spend more time investigating complex threats, improving detection rules, and developing new defenses. Engineers can design more secure systems and automate more components of the security stack. Leadership can make better decisions based on accurate, real-time data. By automating the operational aspects of vulnerability management, organizations empower their people to be more effective and more proactive in defending against cyber threats.

Ultimately, automation in vulnerability management allows for a shift from reactive to proactive security. It enables organizations to respond to vulnerabilities as they emerge, maintain continuous compliance with internal and external requirements, and reduce the window of exposure for critical systems. It brings precision, speed, and repeatability to processes that were once cumbersome and prone to error. In an environment where the volume and sophistication of threats continue to rise, automation is no longer a luxury but a necessity for any organization committed to maintaining a strong and resilient security posture.

Vulnerability Management in CI/CD Pipelines

Vulnerability management in CI/CD pipelines is a critical component of securing modern software development processes. Continuous Integration and Continuous Deployment practices have revolutionized how applications are built, tested, and delivered, allowing teams to push changes rapidly and frequently. While this speed enables innovation and responsiveness, it also introduces security challenges. Each code commit, library inclusion, configuration file, or infrastructure definition has the potential to introduce new vulnerabilities into the environment. In a traditional development cycle, security was often an afterthought, addressed late in the process through manual review or post-deployment scanning. In a CI/CD environment, however, this approach is no longer sustainable. To be effective, vulnerability management must be embedded throughout the pipeline and operate with the same speed, automation, and repeatability as the rest of the DevOps lifecycle.

The integration of security into CI/CD begins with shifting vulnerability detection as far left as possible in the development process. This means incorporating security testing tools that analyze code for vulnerabilities at the time of development and code commit. Static Application Security Testing tools perform deep analysis of source code, identifying common issues such as input validation errors, injection points, and insecure configurations. When integrated into version control platforms, these tools can trigger scans automatically on each commit or pull request, providing developers with immediate feedback. This early detection allows vulnerabilities to be addressed before they reach production and avoids the costly delays associated with last-minute fixes.

The next layer in CI/CD vulnerability management involves dependency scanning, often referred to as Software Composition Analysis. Modern applications rely heavily on third-party libraries and open-source packages, many of which may contain known vulnerabilities. As developers include these dependencies in their codebase, automated tools scan their versions and compare them to vulnerability databases such as the National Vulnerability Database or proprietary threat intelligence feeds. When vulnerable components are detected, the tools issue warnings, suggest updated versions, or even block the build process if the risk is high. By automating this analysis within the pipeline, organizations can maintain visibility over their software supply chain and reduce exposure to vulnerabilities that originate from external sources.

As code is compiled, packaged, and prepared for deployment, additional layers of vulnerability scanning are applied to the build artifacts. For containerized applications, this involves scanning Docker images for outdated or misconfigured base layers, embedded secrets, or packages with known exploits. For virtual machines or infrastructure templates, it means checking for insecure configurations, open ports, or weak authentication policies. These scans are executed automatically as part of the build process and their results are made available to developers and security engineers. If a scan fails due to the presence of critical vulnerabilities, the pipeline can be configured to halt the build and require remediation before progressing further.

Beyond detection, the management of vulnerabilities in CI/CD pipelines also includes structured remediation workflows. When a vulnerability is identified, the system must automatically create a ticket or issue in the organization's tracking system, assign it to the relevant developer or team, and set a due date based on the severity and risk context. These tasks are embedded into existing workflows so that security actions become a natural part of the development process rather than a disruptive add-on. Collaboration between development, operations, and security teams is facilitated through shared visibility and common tooling, enabling faster resolution and reducing friction.

An effective CI/CD vulnerability management strategy also includes the validation of fixes. After a patch is applied or a vulnerable dependency is updated, the system should automatically rerun the relevant security scans to confirm that the issue has been resolved and that no new issues have been introduced. This loop of detection, remediation, and verification creates a reliable and repeatable process that supports continuous delivery without sacrificing security. Furthermore, by maintaining detailed logs of vulnerabilities, actions taken, and outcomes, the system supports auditability and compliance with regulatory requirements or internal security policies.

To ensure that vulnerability management in CI/CD pipelines operates at scale, organizations must embrace automation. Manual review of code, dependencies, and artifacts is not feasible when dozens or hundreds of builds are being executed daily. Automation ensures consistency, reduces human error, and allows teams to keep pace with the rapid iterations demanded by business needs. Security policies can be codified as rules within the pipeline, defining acceptable thresholds for risk, required approvals for exceptions, and mandatory security gates for critical systems. These automated policies enforce governance without slowing down development, striking a balance between agility and control.

Continuous monitoring is another vital element. Even after deployment, applications and infrastructure must be scanned regularly for new vulnerabilities that may emerge post-release. Integrating runtime monitoring tools with CI/CD systems allows for automated alerts when vulnerabilities are discovered in deployed environments. This real-time feedback loop connects production systems back to the development pipeline, triggering new builds or patches as needed. It ensures that security remains a continuous concern, not just a phase in the release cycle.

Training and culture are key to making vulnerability management in CI/CD pipelines successful. Developers must understand the importance of secure coding and how to interpret and act on findings from security tools. Security engineers must understand the development process and build pipelines to provide relevant, actionable feedback. This shared responsibility model is often referred to as DevSecOps, emphasizing the integration of security into every phase of development and deployment. Training programs, security champions, and collaborative incident reviews help reinforce this culture and embed security into the mindset of all teams involved.

Metrics and reporting are essential to measure the effectiveness of vulnerability management within CI/CD. Organizations should track metrics such as the number of vulnerabilities detected per build, average time to remediate, percentage of builds blocked by security issues, and trends over time in dependency risk. These insights inform strategic decisions, identify areas for improvement, and demonstrate the value of the program to executive stakeholders. Automated dashboards can provide real-time views into the security posture of applications, helping teams stay ahead of emerging threats.

As CI/CD becomes the standard model for software delivery, integrating vulnerability management into the pipeline is not optional. It is a fundamental requirement for maintaining secure, reliable, and trustworthy systems. By embedding security into each phase of the development lifecycle, organizations reduce risk, respond to threats faster, and build software that is secure by design. This integration transforms security from a bottleneck into a built-in quality function, enabling teams to innovate confidently in an increasingly hostile digital landscape.

The Role of Artificial Intelligence

The role of artificial intelligence in vulnerability management is growing rapidly as organizations seek to enhance the speed, accuracy, and efficiency of their cybersecurity programs. With the expanding attack surface, the rise of cloud computing, the proliferation of connected devices, and the increasing complexity of enterprise environments, traditional approaches to managing vulnerabilities are no longer sufficient. The sheer volume of data generated by modern systems, from logs and alerts to vulnerability scans and threat intelligence feeds, requires a level of analysis that exceeds human capacity. Artificial intelligence, particularly through the use of machine learning and natural language processing, introduces new capabilities that enable organizations to automate decision-making, identify patterns, and predict risks with a level of speed and precision that was previously unattainable.

At the foundation of AI-driven vulnerability management is the ability to process vast amounts of data in real time. Security environments generate millions of data points every day, including scan results, configuration settings, software inventories, and threat intelligence reports. AI systems can ingest and normalize this data, identifying correlations and anomalies that would be difficult or impossible for human analysts to detect manually. This analysis allows for the automatic classification and prioritization of vulnerabilities based on contextual risk, such as whether an exploit is publicly available, whether the affected asset is exposed to the internet, and whether that asset hosts critical data or services. Instead of relying solely on static severity scores like CVSS, AI can evaluate the actual risk posed to the organization, enabling smarter remediation decisions.

One of the most valuable applications of artificial intelligence is in predictive analytics. By analyzing historical data on past vulnerabilities, incidents, and threat actor behavior, AI models can anticipate which vulnerabilities are most likely to be exploited in the wild. These predictive insights help security teams focus their efforts where they will have the greatest impact, even before a vulnerability is widely known or exploited. For example, if AI models identify that vulnerabilities of a certain type, affecting a particular software vendor, are often targeted by advanced persistent threats within a specific industry, it can automatically flag new vulnerabilities fitting that profile for immediate action. This proactive approach enables organizations to get ahead of attackers rather than reacting after the damage is done.

Artificial intelligence also enhances the efficiency of remediation processes by recommending the most effective and least disruptive fixes for identified vulnerabilities. AI can analyze previous remediation actions and outcomes to suggest whether patching, configuration changes, or compensating controls are most appropriate in a given situation. For organizations with thousands of assets and limited IT resources, this level of guidance is critical in prioritizing work and minimizing business disruption. AI systems can even simulate the impact of proposed changes, ensuring that remediation efforts do not inadvertently introduce new problems or cause service outages.

In addition to operational benefits, AI supports vulnerability management through the automation of routine tasks. Tasks such as data enrichment, ticket generation, asset attribution, and false positive suppression can be handled autonomously by AI-driven systems. When a vulnerability is detected, AI can pull in additional context such as asset criticality, business unit ownership, and usage patterns to fully understand the significance of the finding. It can then create and assign tickets, set appropriate deadlines, and monitor progress without human intervention. This reduces the workload on security and IT teams, speeds up response times, and ensures that vulnerabilities are not forgotten or lost in the system.

Natural language processing, a subset of artificial intelligence, plays an important role in extracting insights from unstructured data sources. Vulnerability advisories, threat intelligence bulletins, security blogs, and social media posts often contain critical information but are not structured in a way that traditional systems can easily process. NLP enables AI to read, interpret, and summarize these sources, automatically flagging relevant findings and integrating them into the organization's vulnerability knowledge base. This continuous stream of contextual information helps teams stay updated on emerging threats, zero-day vulnerabilities, and vendor advisories, even before they are incorporated into official databases.

AI is also transforming the way organizations measure and report on vulnerability management performance. By analyzing trends over time, AI can identify patterns such as recurring vulnerabilities in specific systems, teams that consistently miss remediation deadlines, or dependencies that frequently introduce risk. These insights support continuous improvement initiatives, allowing organizations to refine their development practices, procurement standards, and operational procedures. Executive dashboards powered by AI offer dynamic visualizations of risk, showing real-time metrics and projections based on current data. This empowers leadership to make informed decisions about investments, staffing, and policy changes with a clear understanding of their security posture.

The integration of AI into vulnerability management also contributes to improved incident response. When an exploit is detected in the wild, AI can quickly cross-reference known vulnerabilities in the environment and assess whether any affected assets are exposed. It can simulate attack paths, assess the potential impact, and recommend containment strategies. In some cases, AI systems can even initiate automated response actions, such as isolating compromised systems, blocking malicious traffic, or disabling vulnerable services. This ability to react in real time significantly reduces the window of exposure and helps contain threats before they escalate into major incidents.

Despite its many advantages, the use of artificial intelligence in vulnerability management is not without challenges. AI systems require high-quality data to function effectively, and biases or inaccuracies in the input can lead to flawed conclusions. Organizations must ensure that their data sources are reliable, current, and comprehensive. There is also a need for transparency and explainability in AI-driven decisions. Security teams must understand why a particular vulnerability was prioritized or why a specific remediation was recommended in order to maintain trust in the system and ensure accountability. Furthermore, AI should be viewed as an augmentation of human capability, not a replacement. Human oversight remains essential for interpreting complex findings, managing exceptions, and making judgment calls in situations where nuance and experience are critical.

Artificial intelligence offers a powerful enhancement to vulnerability management by enabling faster detection, smarter prioritization, and more efficient remediation of security weaknesses. As threat landscapes continue to evolve and the volume of data continues to grow, AI will become increasingly indispensable in helping organizations maintain robust and responsive security programs. By combining the analytical power of machines with the strategic insight of human experts, organizations can create a vulnerability management framework that is not only reactive but also adaptive, predictive, and resilient against the challenges of tomorrow.

Prioritizing Business Risk Over Technical Risk

Prioritizing business risk over technical risk is a fundamental shift in how organizations approach vulnerability management, particularly as cybersecurity moves from being a purely technical discipline to a strategic business function. While technical severity scores, such as those provided by CVSS, offer valuable insight into the potential damage a vulnerability could cause from a system perspective, they do not always align with the actual impact that the vulnerability would have on the organization's operations, reputation, regulatory obligations, or financial health. Treating all vulnerabilities based on technical risk alone often results in wasted effort, misaligned priorities, and a false sense of security. By focusing on business risk, organizations ensure that their limited security resources are used where they matter most—protecting the systems and data that are critical to the organization's success and continuity.

The difference between technical and business risk lies in context. Technical risk evaluates the inherent characteristics of a vulnerability, such as ease of exploitation, required privileges, and potential for system compromise. Business risk, on the other hand, considers the broader implications of that vulnerability within the specific operational environment. For example, a low-complexity remote code execution vulnerability on a server that processes millions of dollars in transactions daily represents a far greater risk to the business than a critical vulnerability on a system that is isolated, non-critical, and protected by multiple layers of controls. Business risk factors include the value of the asset to the organization, the sensitivity of the data it handles, the role it plays in customer trust, and the regulatory implications of a breach involving that asset.

Prioritizing business risk requires organizations to maintain an accurate and detailed inventory of assets, along with their classifications and dependencies. Without knowing which systems are mission-critical, which databases store sensitive customer information, and which applications support revenue-generating services, it is impossible to contextualize vulnerabilities appropriately. Asset management must be tightly integrated with vulnerability management so that when a flaw is detected, it is immediately associated with a business function. This integration enables security teams to quickly assess the potential business impact of a vulnerability and determine whether it warrants urgent attention or can be scheduled for routine maintenance.

Risk-based prioritization also demands collaboration between security professionals and business leaders. Too often, cybersecurity decisions are made in isolation, based solely on technical metrics, without input from those who understand the operational realities of the organization. Engaging stakeholders across departments, including finance, operations, legal, and customer service, helps build a more comprehensive understanding of which systems are most vital and what the true consequences of an incident would be. This cross-functional input ensures that the prioritization process reflects real-world concerns, such as contractual obligations, service-level agreements, or the potential for regulatory fines or public backlash.

Another essential component of business risk prioritization is threat intelligence. Understanding which vulnerabilities are actively being exploited in the wild, which threat actors are targeting your industry, and what techniques they are using allows organizations to better assess the likelihood of an attack. Even if a vulnerability is technically severe, if it is not being exploited and exists on a system with robust compensating controls, the business risk may be low. Conversely, a medium-severity flaw that is part of an active ransomware campaign targeting your sector may pose a much higher business risk. Integrating real-time threat intelligence into the prioritization process helps ensure that the organization's efforts are aligned with the evolving threat landscape.

Remediation strategies must also be shaped by business risk. Patching a vulnerability may require downtime, testing, or changes to applications that could disrupt business operations. When business risk is the guiding principle, decisions about remediation timelines, mitigation approaches, and exception handling are made with an understanding of the trade-offs. In some cases, it may be acceptable to delay a patch if compensating controls such as network segmentation, access restrictions, or monitoring are sufficient to manage the risk. In other cases, immediate action is necessary even if it causes temporary disruption. These decisions are best made with a clear understanding of the business context, not just the technical details.

Reporting is another area where the focus on business risk becomes valuable. Executives and board members are rarely interested in the number of vulnerabilities discovered or the technical details of a specific exploit. They want to know whether the business is at risk, how that risk is being managed, and whether the organization is in compliance with relevant laws and standards. Framing vulnerability management metrics in terms of business impact—such as the number of unresolved high-risk vulnerabilities on critical systems, or the average time to remediate flaws that affect customer-facing applications—helps leadership make informed decisions and allocate resources appropriately.

Organizations that prioritize business risk over technical risk also build stronger relationships between IT, security, and the business. When security teams demonstrate that they understand the business's goals and constraints, they are more likely to receive support, cooperation, and funding. Rather than being seen as an obstacle or a cost center, security becomes a strategic enabler, helping the organization manage uncertainty, protect value, and innovate with confidence. This alignment fosters a culture where risk is understood, shared, and managed collaboratively across the enterprise.

Technology plays an important role in enabling business risk prioritization. Modern vulnerability management platforms offer features such as asset criticality tagging, business unit mapping, and automated risk scoring that incorporates both technical and contextual data. These tools help security teams quickly visualize their risk exposure and prioritize remediation based on the potential impact to the organization. Integrating these platforms with configuration management databases, threat intelligence feeds, and ticketing systems further enhances their ability to deliver actionable insights at scale.

Ultimately, prioritizing business risk over technical risk is about making smarter decisions. It ensures that the right vulnerabilities are addressed at the right time, not because they have the highest CVSS score, but because they pose the greatest threat to the organization's mission. It aligns security efforts with strategic objectives, improves the effectiveness of vulnerability management programs, and builds resilience in the face of an increasingly complex and hostile digital environment. This approach recognizes that not all vulnerabilities are created equal and that the true measure of risk lies in understanding the potential business consequences of a security failure. By placing business risk at the center of the decision-making process, organizations can better protect what matters most.

Third-Party and Supply Chain Vulnerabilities

Third-party and supply chain vulnerabilities have become one of the most critical and complex challenges in modern cybersecurity. As organizations increasingly rely on external vendors, contractors, cloud providers, software components, and service integrations to support operations, they also expand their exposure to threats that originate beyond their direct control. These dependencies introduce indirect paths for attackers to infiltrate environments, often exploiting weaknesses in partners or software dependencies rather than targeting an organization head-on. The interconnected nature of today's digital supply chains means that a vulnerability in one link can ripple across multiple businesses, industries, and even national infrastructures. Understanding, identifying, and managing these risks is essential for protecting both operational integrity and customer trust.

A key factor in the growing risk from third parties is the increasing complexity of the supply chain itself. Organizations now use a multitude of vendors for specialized tasks, ranging from payment processors and logistics platforms to managed service providers and data analytics firms. Each of these entities may have access to sensitive data, internal systems, or production environments. Furthermore, many organizations rely heavily on third-party software, including open-source libraries and commercial applications, to build and run their products and services. These third-party elements are often deeply embedded within systems, making them difficult to inventory, monitor, and patch. As a result, vulnerabilities in these external components can remain undetected for long periods, creating persistent security gaps.

One of the most well-known examples of supply chain compromise is the case of attackers injecting malicious code into legitimate software updates. This tactic exploits the trust relationship between a software provider and its users, allowing attackers to deliver backdoors or malware to thousands of targets through a single breach. In such cases, even highly secure organizations become vulnerable simply because they installed a compromised update from a trusted vendor. These attacks are particularly dangerous because they often go unnoticed for extended periods and may bypass traditional security controls. The SolarWinds breach is a notable illustration of this tactic, where attackers inserted malicious code into a widely used IT management platform, compromising multiple government and private-sector networks worldwide.

Managing third-party and supply chain vulnerabilities requires a holistic approach that includes both proactive assessment and continuous monitoring. The first step is to gain visibility into all third-party relationships and software dependencies. This includes identifying which vendors have access to internal networks, which applications rely on external libraries, and where third-party integrations intersect with sensitive data or critical operations. A comprehensive vendor inventory should include details such as the type of service provided, data access permissions, authentication mechanisms, contract terms, and incident response capabilities. Similarly, a software bill of materials, or SBOM, provides a detailed list of all components used in an application, including open-source dependencies and nested libraries. These tools help organizations understand where third-party risk exists and how it propagates through their systems.

Assessment is the next layer of defense. Before engaging with a new vendor, organizations should conduct security due diligence that evaluates the vendor's cybersecurity posture, data protection policies, and compliance with relevant standards. This process may include security questionnaires, third-party audits, vulnerability assessments, and contractual obligations for breach notification and data handling. Vendors should also be required to demonstrate that they perform regular security testing, patch management, and monitoring of their own supply chains. For software products, static and dynamic analysis can help identify embedded vulnerabilities, while code review and cryptographic signing can provide assurance of software integrity. These assessments should not be a one-time exercise but part of an ongoing vendor management program that re-evaluates risk periodically.

Despite best efforts, vulnerabilities in third-party systems will still occur. That is why continuous monitoring is essential. Organizations must implement systems that detect anomalous behavior associated with third-party access, such as unusual data transfers, unauthorized login attempts, or configuration changes. Network segmentation can help limit the potential damage from a compromised vendor account, ensuring that attackers cannot move laterally through internal systems. Integration with security information and event management platforms allows for correlation of events and faster detection of supply chain attacks. Endpoint detection and response tools can identify unusual activity originating from third-party software and initiate automated containment procedures.

Incident response plans must also account for third-party and supply chain incidents. Traditional response protocols often assume that the threat originates internally or through direct network exposure. However, supply chain attacks require coordination with external stakeholders, legal teams, and public relations. When a vulnerability or breach is discovered in a third-party service, organizations must quickly assess whether they are affected, what data or systems are at risk, and how to mitigate the impact. Response plans should include pre-established lines of communication with vendors, clear escalation paths, and legal frameworks that define responsibilities. Public disclosure may also be necessary depending on regulatory requirements and the severity of the incident.

Regulatory and industry frameworks are increasingly focusing on third-party risk as a key compliance area. Standards such as NIST SP 800-161, the EU's Digital Operational Resilience Act, and ISO/IEC 27036 provide guidance on managing supply chain security. Additionally, regulators in finance, healthcare, and critical infrastructure sectors are introducing stricter requirements for vendor risk management and supply chain transparency. Non-compliance with these frameworks can result in fines, loss of licenses, or reputational harm. As a result, organizations must ensure that their vulnerability management programs are aligned with both legal expectations and best practices for third-party oversight.

Technology can assist in managing third-party vulnerabilities by automating discovery, assessment, and monitoring tasks. Tools that track software dependencies can automatically alert teams when a component becomes vulnerable. Threat intelligence platforms can monitor for emerging risks in the supply chain, such as new attack campaigns targeting a specific vendor or product. Vendor risk management solutions can streamline the assessment process and maintain documentation for audits. However, technology alone is not enough. Effective third-party risk management also requires strong governance, executive support, and a culture of shared responsibility across the enterprise.

Ultimately, managing third-party and supply chain vulnerabilities is not just a technical challenge but a strategic one. It involves understanding the broader ecosystem in which an organization operates and recognizing that security is only as strong as its weakest link. By building transparency, enforcing accountability, and embedding security into the selection and monitoring of all external dependencies, organizations can significantly reduce their exposure to these growing threats. The goal is not to eliminate all risk—an impossible task—but to manage it intelligently, detect issues quickly, and respond with speed and confidence when the supply chain becomes the battleground.

Challenges in Large Enterprises

Managing vulnerabilities in large enterprises presents a distinct set of challenges that stem from the scale, complexity, and organizational structure inherent to these environments. Unlike small or mid-sized businesses, large enterprises often consist of thousands of endpoints, hundreds of business units, multiple geographic regions, and a vast array of interconnected systems, cloud services, legacy infrastructure, and third-party integrations. Each of these components introduces its own risks and operational considerations, making vulnerability management not just a technical task but a strategic initiative that must be planned, coordinated, and executed across diverse teams and domains. The size of the organization itself becomes a barrier to visibility, agility, and consistency, requiring a high degree of process maturity, automation, and cross-functional collaboration.

One of the most pressing challenges in large enterprises is asset visibility. In a sprawling environment, it can be extraordinarily difficult to maintain a complete and accurate inventory of all assets that need to be scanned and secured. Systems are constantly being added, removed, virtualized, or moved to cloud platforms. Departments may operate with a degree of autonomy, leading to the deployment of shadow IT systems that fall outside of centralized oversight. Without knowing exactly what assets exist and where they are, it is impossible to scan for vulnerabilities effectively or prioritize remediation. Even when asset discovery tools are in place, they may struggle to reconcile disparate naming conventions, duplicate entries, and inconsistent metadata, leading to gaps in coverage or misaligned risk assessments.

The diversity of systems in large enterprises also complicates vulnerability management. A single organization may run multiple operating systems, versions, applications, and configurations across on-premise data centers, private clouds, and public cloud platforms. Legacy systems that are critical to business operations may not support modern security tools or may require downtime to patch, which is often difficult to schedule. In some cases, there may be custom-built applications or industrial control systems that have no vendor support and cannot be easily updated. These complexities mean that standard scanning tools may not work uniformly across the environment, and remediation strategies must be customized for each platform. This diversity requires specialized knowledge and careful planning, which can slow down response times and increase operational overhead.

Organizational structure is another major barrier in large enterprises. Different business units often operate independently, with separate IT and security teams, budgets, tools, and processes. This decentralization can lead to inconsistent security postures, duplicated efforts, and poor communication. One team may be diligent about applying patches and scanning regularly, while another may lack the resources or incentives to prioritize security. Governance frameworks are necessary to establish enterprise-wide standards, but enforcing these standards across a fragmented organization requires political capital, executive support, and ongoing education. In many cases, security teams must act as both enforcers and collaborators, building trust and demonstrating value in order to gain buy-in from business units that may view security as an obstacle rather than an enabler.

The scale of operations in large enterprises also means that even simple tasks become complex. Rolling out a patch to hundreds of thousands of devices involves coordination across multiple change management systems, approval workflows, testing environments, and rollback plans. Any mistake can cause widespread disruption, leading to a culture of risk aversion that delays remediation. Additionally, large organizations must contend with maintenance windows, service-level agreements, and high-availability requirements that limit when and how changes can be made. Balancing the need for speed with the demand for stability is a constant tension in vulnerability management. Automated patching solutions can help, but they must be implemented with careful safeguards to avoid unintended consequences.

Data overload is another challenge. Vulnerability scans in large environments generate massive amounts of data. Filtering through this data to identify actionable risks, eliminate false positives, and prioritize remediation can overwhelm security teams. Without robust filtering, correlation, and reporting capabilities, teams may spend valuable time chasing low-risk vulnerabilities while missing the ones that pose genuine threats. Data must be enriched with context, such as asset criticality, user access levels, and exposure to the internet, in order to be meaningful. This requires integration between vulnerability management tools and other systems like asset management databases, SIEMs, and configuration management platforms. Building and maintaining these integrations at scale is resource-intensive but essential for effective decision-making.

Another issue that large enterprises face is compliance and audit pressure. Many are subject to multiple regulatory frameworks, such as GDPR, HIPAA, PCI DSS, SOX, and industry-specific standards. Each of these may impose different requirements for vulnerability scanning, patch timelines, documentation, and reporting. Managing compliance across jurisdictions, business lines, and technology stacks adds another layer of complexity. Security teams must ensure that their vulnerability management practices are not only effective but also auditable. This involves producing detailed records of scans, findings, remediation actions, exceptions, and approvals. In large enterprises, compliance reporting can become a full-time job and often requires dedicated staff and tools to manage effectively.

Human resource challenges also come into play. Recruiting and retaining skilled cybersecurity professionals is difficult in any environment, but in large enterprises, the scale and scope of work can lead to burnout and turnover. The demand for specialized skills, such as vulnerability analysis, penetration testing, and secure software development, often exceeds supply. Internal training programs, knowledge sharing, and career development opportunities are necessary to build a sustainable security workforce. In addition, the complexity of the environment means that institutional knowledge is critical. Losing experienced staff can result in knowledge gaps that take months to fill.

Large enterprises must also deal with the challenge of aligning security with business objectives. Security initiatives are often seen as cost centers, competing with revenue-generating projects for funding and attention. Demonstrating the business value of vulnerability management—such as preventing breaches, avoiding regulatory penalties, and maintaining customer trust—is essential to securing executive support. Metrics that translate technical risk into business impact are vital for gaining visibility at the board level. Security leaders must be able to articulate how vulnerabilities in specific systems could disrupt operations, damage the brand, or expose the company to legal liability.

Despite these challenges, large enterprises also have advantages that can be leveraged to improve vulnerability management. They have the resources to invest in enterprise-grade tools, hire specialized talent, and build out mature security operations centers. They can form partnerships with vendors, participate in industry information-sharing forums, and lead innovation in threat detection and response. What matters most is how these resources are organized, prioritized, and executed. With a clear strategy, strong leadership, and a focus on collaboration, even the largest organizations can manage vulnerabilities effectively and build resilience in a constantly changing threat landscape.

Securing Remote Work Infrastructure

Securing remote work infrastructure has become a critical priority for organizations worldwide as the traditional boundaries of corporate networks have expanded beyond office walls. The shift to remote and hybrid work models, accelerated by global events and technological advancements, has brought significant flexibility and productivity gains but also introduced a complex set of security challenges. Employees now access corporate resources from home offices, public networks, and mobile devices, often using personal hardware that is not subject to centralized control or standardized security configurations. As a result, the attack surface has grown exponentially, and traditional perimeter-based security models are no longer sufficient to protect sensitive data, systems, and services.

One of the most significant risks in remote work environments is the use of unmanaged or poorly secured endpoints. Employees may connect to company resources using personal laptops, smartphones, or tablets that lack enterprise-grade security protections such as endpoint detection and response, centralized patch management, or disk encryption. These devices may also have outdated software, vulnerable applications, or malware infections that can be used as entry points into corporate systems. To mitigate this risk, organizations must implement strict endpoint security policies that include the use of managed devices, mandatory antivirus solutions, disk encryption, and automated patching. Where personal devices are permitted, they should be subject to mobile device management or bring-your-own-device security policies that enforce minimum standards for access.

Another critical component of remote work security is secure connectivity. Employees must access corporate systems over the internet, which is inherently insecure. Virtual private networks (VPNs) have traditionally been used to encrypt traffic and authenticate users, but they present limitations when scaled to support an entire remote workforce. VPNs can become performance bottlenecks, and if compromised, they may provide attackers with broad access to internal systems. As an alternative or complement to VPNs, many organizations have adopted zero trust network access models. Zero trust enforces strict identity verification and access controls based on contextual factors such as device health, user behavior, and geolocation. Rather than assuming that a connection is safe because it originates from a known network, zero trust evaluates each request individually and allows access only to the resources explicitly needed by the user.

Identity and access management is central to securing remote work infrastructure. Strong authentication methods, such as multifactor authentication (MFA), are no longer optional. Passwords alone cannot protect against phishing, credential stuffing, or brute-force attacks. MFA requires users to provide a second factor, such as a smartphone notification, hardware token, or biometric verification, which significantly reduces the likelihood of unauthorized access. In addition to enforcing MFA, organizations must implement least privilege access controls, ensuring that users have only the permissions necessary for their roles. Role-based access control, just-in-time access provisioning, and regular access reviews help prevent privilege creep and limit the damage that can be done if an account is compromised.

Securing collaboration tools is another essential task in remote work environments. Video conferencing platforms, file-sharing services, and instant messaging tools are vital for communication and productivity but can become vectors for data leakage, account hijacking, or unauthorized access if not properly secured. Organizations must ensure that these tools are configured with strong access controls, encrypted communications, and logging capabilities. Employees should be trained on the proper use of these tools, including avoiding the sharing of sensitive information in unencrypted channels, securing meeting invites with passwords, and recognizing phishing attempts that mimic legitimate collaboration tools.

Visibility and monitoring remain foundational elements of any security strategy and are particularly important in remote work settings. Traditional monitoring tools designed for centralized networks may not provide adequate visibility into activities occurring on remote endpoints or cloud services. Organizations must extend their logging and monitoring capabilities to include remote devices, cloud applications, and user behavior. Endpoint detection and response solutions, security information and event management systems, and user and entity behavior analytics can detect anomalies such as unusual login times, access from unrecognized devices, or large file transfers. These tools enable security teams to detect potential breaches quickly and take appropriate action before significant damage occurs.

Data protection is another top priority in remote work infrastructure. Sensitive corporate data may now reside on personal devices, be transferred over public networks, or be stored in third-party cloud platforms. Data loss prevention tools can help enforce policies that restrict the movement of sensitive information, such as blocking file uploads to unauthorized websites or encrypting email attachments. Encryption, both at rest and in transit, ensures that even if data is intercepted or stolen, it cannot be read without the appropriate decryption keys. Organizations must also implement secure backup strategies that protect against ransomware attacks and ensure that critical data can be recovered in the event of a compromise.

Training and awareness are critical components of securing remote work infrastructure. Employees are the first line of defense, and their actions can either strengthen or undermine security efforts. Phishing remains one of the most effective methods for attackers to compromise accounts, especially when employees are working from home and may be distracted or isolated from IT support. Regular security awareness training should cover topics such as recognizing phishing emails, securing home Wi-Fi networks, using strong passwords, and reporting suspicious activity. Simulated phishing campaigns and targeted microlearning sessions can reinforce these lessons and help build a culture of security mindfulness.

Organizations must also plan for incident response in remote work environments. Traditional response plans may assume that IT staff have physical access to affected devices or that users are on a corporate network. In a remote work model, these assumptions no longer hold. Incident response procedures must be updated to include remote containment, investigation, and recovery actions. This may involve remote access tools for forensic analysis, secure communication channels for coordinating responses, and clear guidance for employees on what to do if they suspect a security incident. Having a tested and remote-friendly incident response plan ensures that the organization can react quickly and effectively when threats arise.

Finally, compliance and governance must not be overlooked. Many industries are subject to regulations that require specific security measures, data handling practices, and audit capabilities. Remote work does not exempt organizations from these obligations. Instead, it requires that security controls and documentation be extended to cover remote systems and users. Regular audits, compliance assessments, and policy reviews ensure that remote work practices align with legal and regulatory requirements. By embedding security into every aspect of remote work infrastructure—from endpoints and access to monitoring and response—organizations can maintain strong defenses, support flexible work arrangements, and build resilience in an increasingly digital world.

Role of Security Operations Centers (SOCs)

The role of Security Operations Centers, commonly referred to as SOCs, is fundamental to modern cybersecurity strategy, especially in the context of vulnerability management and threat detection. A SOC acts as the nerve center of an organization's security posture, operating continuously to monitor, detect, analyze, respond to, and recover from cybersecurity incidents. It is both a physical or virtual facility and a team of dedicated professionals whose mission is to safeguard information assets, digital infrastructure, and the continuity of operations. In an age where cyberattacks are not a matter of if but when, the SOC plays a central role in ensuring that threats are discovered early and dealt with swiftly, while also maintaining the integrity of the systems and data under protection.

A well-functioning SOC operates twenty-four hours a day, seven days a week, three hundred sixty-five days a year. This nonstop vigilance is essential because attackers operate around the clock and often use automation to scan, exploit, and breach systems at scale. The SOC is responsible for maintaining this continuous monitoring through a wide range of tools and technologies, including Security Information and Event Management systems, intrusion detection and prevention systems, endpoint detection and response platforms, and log aggregation solutions. These technologies collect and analyze data from across the enterprise, from network traffic and user activity to system logs and application behavior, producing millions of data points daily. The SOC's job is to sift through this data, identify anomalies, and differentiate legitimate activity from indicators of compromise.

Vulnerability management is one of the SOC's core responsibilities. Although vulnerability discovery may originate from specialized scanning teams or development teams, the SOC is often the hub where vulnerability data is aggregated, contextualized, and acted upon. The SOC helps prioritize vulnerabilities by combining internal asset criticality with external threat intelligence, exploit availability, and exposure. This information is used to guide remediation efforts and to alert appropriate teams when a vulnerability represents an imminent risk. In many cases, the SOC is responsible for correlating vulnerability information with real-time events to determine whether a known vulnerability is being actively exploited in the environment. If suspicious activity is detected on a system with a high-risk vulnerability, the SOC can quickly escalate the incident for containment and investigation.

The SOC team is typically composed of several tiers of analysts, each with increasing levels of expertise and responsibility. Tier one analysts are on the front lines, triaging alerts, reviewing logs, and escalating events that require deeper investigation. Tier two analysts conduct more in-depth analysis, investigating the root cause of alerts, mapping out attack chains, and applying their knowledge of the threat landscape to determine the extent of the threat. Tier three analysts or incident responders are responsible for managing complex or high-severity incidents, coordinating containment and remediation efforts, and performing forensic analysis when needed. In more advanced SOCs, threat hunters and intelligence analysts proactively search for hidden threats using hypothesis-driven investigations and knowledge of attacker tactics, techniques, and procedures.

One of the most important capabilities of the SOC is its ability to respond quickly and effectively to security incidents. When a potential breach is detected, the SOC coordinates the response, isolates affected systems, blocks malicious traffic, and ensures that evidence is preserved for further analysis. This rapid response is essential for minimizing damage, preventing lateral movement, and protecting sensitive data. The SOC maintains detailed runbooks and playbooks that guide analysts through standardized response procedures, ensuring that no steps are missed and that responses are consistent across incidents. Automation also plays a role here, enabling the SOC to contain threats using predefined workflows that can quarantine systems, disable accounts, or trigger alerts without requiring manual intervention.

Communication and coordination are also central to the SOC's role. The SOC serves as the central point of contact during a security incident, interfacing with IT teams, business units, legal departments, and executive leadership. Clear communication ensures that stakeholders are informed, that the impact of an incident is properly assessed, and that response efforts are aligned with organizational priorities. In regulated industries, the SOC also supports compliance by ensuring that incidents are documented, reported, and resolved in accordance with applicable laws and standards. The ability to produce detailed incident reports, audit logs, and timelines is essential for meeting regulatory obligations and for learning from past incidents.

In addition to its reactive role, the SOC also plays a proactive role in improving security posture. This includes identifying trends in attack data, recommending security improvements, and supporting initiatives like red team and penetration testing exercises. The SOC provides feedback on which controls are effective, which systems are frequently targeted, and which vulnerabilities recur over time. This intelligence supports continuous improvement, allowing organizations to adapt their defenses based on real-world data. The SOC may also assist in awareness training, vulnerability scanning, threat modeling, and architecture reviews, acting as a security advisor to the broader organization.

The evolution of the SOC has also been influenced by the move to cloud infrastructure, hybrid environments, and the growing need for scalability and flexibility. Modern SOCs must monitor not only on-premise systems but also cloud-native platforms, SaaS applications, containerized workloads, and remote users. This expanded scope requires new tools, new skills, and a deeper integration with cloud service providers. Cloud security posture management tools, cloud-native SIEMs, and API-based monitoring solutions have become critical to extending the SOC's reach into the cloud. As digital transformation continues, SOCs must evolve to maintain visibility and control across this increasingly decentralized and complex environment.

Staffing and skills are also major considerations for SOCs. The demand for cybersecurity professionals far exceeds supply, and maintaining a high-functioning SOC requires a blend of technical expertise, analytical ability, and operational discipline. Burnout is a common issue, particularly among tier one analysts who deal with a high volume of repetitive alerts. To address this, organizations must invest in automation, career development, and mental wellness programs. Advanced SOCs also integrate artificial intelligence and machine learning to reduce noise, prioritize alerts, and uncover threats that traditional rule-based systems might miss. This use of technology enables SOCs to focus human talent on the highest-value tasks while improving overall accuracy and response speed.

Ultimately, the role of the Security Operations Center is to serve as the guardian of the organization's digital environment. It brings together people, processes, and technology to defend against an ever-evolving threat landscape. Through continuous monitoring, timely response, and strategic analysis, the SOC ensures that security is not just reactive but anticipatory. In doing so, it provides the organization with the confidence to operate, innovate, and grow in a digital world where the cost of inaction is greater than ever. The SOC is more than a technical team; it is the embodiment of the organization's commitment to vigilance, resilience, and trust in the face of constant cyber risk.

Integrating Vulnerability Management with SIEM

Integrating vulnerability management with Security Information and Event Management systems is an essential evolution for organizations aiming to build a proactive, intelligent, and risk-based security strategy. SIEM platforms are designed to aggregate, correlate, and analyze data from a wide range of sources, including logs, security alerts, network traffic, and user behavior. By integrating vulnerability management data into SIEM systems, organizations can add critical context that enhances their ability to detect, prioritize, and respond to threats based not only on observed events but also on the known weaknesses within their environment. This integration transforms static vulnerability data into dynamic, actionable intelligence that supports both security operations and broader risk management efforts.

One of the primary benefits of integrating vulnerability management with SIEM is the enrichment of alerts and event data with vulnerability context. When a SIEM detects unusual activity, such as a series of failed login attempts or suspicious outbound traffic, the addition of vulnerability information can drastically change the response strategy. For example, if the system generating the alerts is known to have an unpatched remote code execution vulnerability, the likelihood that the activity is malicious and poses a high risk is significantly increased. Conversely, if the system is fully patched and hardened, the same event might be deprioritized or treated as a false positive. This contextual awareness allows security analysts to focus their attention and resources where they are most needed.

Another important aspect of integration is the ability to correlate real-time threat indicators with vulnerability data. SIEM platforms excel at identifying patterns across vast amounts of data, but without knowledge of which assets are vulnerable, they cannot determine which threats are most likely to succeed. When vulnerability data is imported into the SIEM, it becomes possible to map indicators of compromise to known vulnerabilities and identify exploitation attempts in progress. This correlation not only speeds up detection but also improves accuracy by reducing false positives and enabling more informed decision-making. Analysts are no longer responding to isolated events but are instead seeing the full picture of how a threat actor may be attempting to exploit a specific weakness in the system.

The integration also enhances incident response capabilities. When an incident is escalated within the SIEM, the availability of vulnerability data allows responders to quickly assess the risk and determine the most appropriate containment and remediation actions. For example, if a compromised system is known to be affected by a critical vulnerability with an available exploit, immediate isolation may be necessary to prevent lateral movement or data exfiltration. The SIEM can also automate certain response actions based on this data, such as creating a high-priority ticket, notifying relevant teams, or triggering workflows in other security tools. This level of automation and coordination significantly reduces the time to respond and helps contain threats before they escalate into major incidents.

Integrating vulnerability management data into the SIEM also supports better reporting and compliance. Security leaders need to understand not only how many vulnerabilities exist in the environment but also how those vulnerabilities relate to real-world threats and organizational risk. SIEM dashboards can display key metrics such as the number of exploitable vulnerabilities actively targeted by attackers, the percentage of critical systems with unresolved vulnerabilities, and the average time to patch. These insights provide a more comprehensive view of the organization's security posture and enable data-driven decisions. They also help demonstrate due diligence to auditors, regulators, and executives by showing that the organization is actively correlating threat data with known risks and taking appropriate action.

To successfully integrate vulnerability management with SIEM, organizations must address several technical and operational considerations. First, they need to ensure that their vulnerability management tools are capable of exporting data in a format compatible with the SIEM. This may involve using APIs, connectors, or data normalization layers that transform vulnerability scan results into structured, standardized events. The data must include relevant fields such as asset identifiers, CVE numbers, severity scores, patch status, and exploitability information. Without accurate and consistent data, the value of the integration is diminished, and correlations may produce misleading results.

Second, asset identity management is critical. Vulnerability scanners and SIEM systems often use different identifiers for systems, such as IP addresses, hostnames, or MAC addresses. If these identifiers do not align, it becomes difficult to correlate events accurately. Organizations must implement asset correlation strategies that unify these identifiers across tools and ensure that all systems are tracked consistently. This may require integration with configuration management databases, asset inventories, or endpoint detection and response platforms that serve as sources of truth for asset data.

Third, organizations must tune their SIEM correlation rules to incorporate vulnerability data effectively. This involves creating logic that elevates the priority of alerts involving vulnerable systems, highlights activity associated with known exploits, and suppresses alerts on fully remediated systems. Correlation rules must be tested, validated, and updated regularly to reflect changes in the environment, new threat intelligence, and updated vulnerability assessments. This ongoing tuning process ensures that the SIEM remains effective as both a detection and prioritization tool.

From an organizational standpoint, integrating vulnerability data into the SIEM promotes greater collaboration between security operations, IT, and vulnerability management teams. It breaks down silos by creating a shared view of risk and encouraging joint ownership of detection, remediation, and reporting processes. Security teams can provide context on threat activity, while IT teams offer insight into patch management constraints and operational priorities. This alignment leads to more realistic remediation timelines, better resource allocation, and fewer misunderstandings about what constitutes an urgent or high-impact issue.

The integration also supports more effective threat hunting and proactive defense strategies. Analysts can query the SIEM for systems with specific vulnerabilities that are known to be targeted by threat actors, allowing them to investigate signs of compromise before an incident is formally detected. They can also monitor for signs of exploitation of newly discovered vulnerabilities, ensuring that zero-day risks are addressed quickly and comprehensively. In this way, the SIEM becomes not just a reactive tool but a forward-looking platform that supports continuous improvement and threat anticipation.

Ultimately, integrating vulnerability management with SIEM transforms vulnerability data from a static list of weaknesses into a living component of the organization's threat detection and response framework. It allows for the real-time application of context to security events, drives smarter decisions, and enables faster, more effective incident response. By uniting these two critical components of cybersecurity, organizations create a more holistic and resilient approach to managing risk in a threat landscape that demands speed, precision, and constant vigilance. This integration is not simply a technical exercise but a strategic initiative that empowers security teams to stay ahead of attackers and protect what matters most.

Lessons from Real-World Breaches

The study of real-world breaches offers invaluable insights into the weaknesses that exist in cybersecurity practices, particularly in vulnerability management. These incidents expose not just technical flaws but also procedural gaps, organizational shortcomings, and missed opportunities for prevention. By examining how breaches occurred, what vulnerabilities were exploited, how attackers moved through systems, and what consequences followed, security professionals can better understand the multifaceted nature of modern threats and refine their defenses accordingly. Real-world breaches serve as case studies that highlight the urgent need for proactive security, effective patch management, comprehensive monitoring, and cross-team collaboration. They reveal recurring themes and patterns that continue to plague organizations across all industries, regardless of size, maturity, or regulatory environment.

One of the most consistent lessons from real-world breaches is the danger of unpatched known vulnerabilities. Many high-profile attacks have exploited vulnerabilities that had been publicly disclosed and for which patches were already available. In some cases, these vulnerabilities remained unpatched for months or even years, despite their severity and the existence of published exploits. The Equifax breach, for example, was traced to a vulnerability in Apache Struts, a web application framework. A patch for the flaw had been released months earlier, yet the system remained exposed. Attackers exploited this weakness to access sensitive personal data of nearly 150 million individuals. This incident underscores the importance of timely patching and the need for accurate asset management to ensure that all vulnerable systems are identified and addressed quickly.

Another recurring theme is the exploitation of default configurations, weak credentials, or exposed administrative interfaces. In numerous breaches, attackers gained initial access through internet-facing systems that were misconfigured or inadequately protected. In the case of the Colonial Pipeline attack, for instance, the breach was reportedly initiated through a compromised VPN account that lacked multifactor authentication. This allowed attackers to bypass perimeter defenses and install ransomware on internal systems. The lesson here is that even seemingly small oversights—like failing to enforce multifactor authentication or leaving default credentials in place—can have devastating consequences. Organizations must prioritize secure configuration management, enforce strong access controls, and regularly audit systems for exposure.

Supply chain compromises have also become a significant source of breaches, with attackers targeting third-party software providers or service vendors to reach their ultimate victims. The SolarWinds breach is a notable example, where attackers inserted malicious code into a software update for the Orion platform, a tool used by thousands of organizations worldwide. When customers installed the compromised update, they inadvertently opened backdoors into their own networks. This attack demonstrated the importance of securing the software supply chain, implementing code integrity verification, and monitoring for anomalous behavior even in trusted applications. It also highlighted the need for organizations to assess the security practices of their vendors and to have contingency plans for managing third-party risks.

Lateral movement within compromised networks is another key lesson. Once inside, attackers often spend weeks or even months exploring systems, escalating privileges, and exfiltrating data without detection. In the Target breach, attackers initially compromised HVAC vendor credentials, then moved laterally through the network until they reached the point-of-sale systems, where they installed malware to capture customer payment data. This breach illustrates how a single vulnerability, when combined with insufficient network segmentation and lack of monitoring, can lead to a full-scale compromise. Effective defenses require not just perimeter protection but internal controls, behavioral monitoring, and the principle of least privilege to limit what an attacker can do once inside.

Insider threats and social engineering tactics are also frequently observed in real-world breaches. Phishing remains one of the most common initial attack vectors, exploiting human error rather than technical weaknesses. Breaches at companies like Sony Pictures and RSA began with phishing emails that tricked employees into opening malicious attachments or clicking on links that installed malware. These incidents emphasize the need for ongoing security awareness training, simulated phishing exercises, and layered defenses that can detect and contain threats that bypass user vigilance. No technology can fully eliminate human error, but education and practice can reduce its likelihood and impact.

Another important lesson is the necessity of robust incident detection and response capabilities. Many breached organizations discovered the intrusion only after significant damage had already been done. Some were notified by external parties, such as law enforcement or security researchers, indicating that their internal detection mechanisms had failed. Delayed detection allows attackers more time to steal data, cause disruption, or install additional tools for future access. The average dwell time—the duration between initial compromise and detection—remains alarmingly high across industries. This highlights the importance of investing in tools and processes that support real-time monitoring, threat hunting, and rapid response. Security Information and Event Management systems, endpoint detection and response tools, and 24/7 Security Operations Centers can all play a role in reducing detection time and improving outcomes.

The post-breach response also provides crucial lessons. Communication breakdowns, delayed disclosures, and poor public messaging can worsen the reputational damage and legal consequences of a breach. Companies that respond transparently and swiftly tend to recover more effectively, while those that appear evasive or unprepared often face increased scrutiny and longer-term fallout. The Marriott and Yahoo breaches both involved delayed disclosure of incidents affecting hundreds of millions of users, leading to regulatory investigations and erosion of customer trust. These examples underscore the importance of having an incident response plan that includes clear communication strategies, defined roles and responsibilities, and compliance with breach notification requirements.

From real-world breaches, it is also clear that cybersecurity is not solely a technical issue but a governance issue. Executive leadership must be engaged in cybersecurity strategy, funding, and risk management. Breaches frequently reveal systemic issues such as lack of investment in security, fragmented responsibilities, or misalignment between IT and business objectives. Organizations that embed cybersecurity into their culture, governance, and decision-making processes are better equipped to prevent, detect, and respond to breaches. Regular board-level reporting, security risk assessments, and executive-level participation in incident response exercises help ensure that security is viewed as a strategic priority rather than an afterthought.

Ultimately, the lessons from real-world breaches remind us that vulnerabilities are not just weaknesses in code but reflections of broader organizational behavior. They reveal gaps in visibility, breakdowns in process, and underestimation of threats. By learning from the past and understanding how breaches occur, organizations can strengthen their defenses, reduce risk, and build the resilience necessary to withstand the next wave of cyber threats. Each breach is a costly but valuable opportunity to reassess assumptions, close gaps, and move toward a more mature and adaptive cybersecurity posture.

Internal vs External Vulnerability Assessments

Internal and external vulnerability assessments are two fundamental components of a comprehensive vulnerability management program. Each serves a distinct purpose and provides unique insights into an organization's security posture. While both aim to identify and mitigate weaknesses in systems and configurations, they do so from different perspectives and within different scopes. Understanding the differences between these two approaches, and recognizing how they complement one another, is critical for reducing risk, protecting assets, and ensuring that both perimeter and internal systems are adequately defended against evolving threats.

An external vulnerability assessment is conducted from outside the organization's network perimeter. The purpose of this assessment is to simulate how a potential attacker, who does not have authorized access, might identify and exploit vulnerabilities exposed to the public internet. External assessments typically focus on internet-facing systems, such as web servers, email gateways, DNS servers, VPN endpoints, and any applications or services that are accessible remotely. These assessments identify issues like open ports, outdated software, exposed services, misconfigured firewalls, and common vulnerabilities that could be leveraged by an attacker to gain a foothold in the network.

The external assessment reflects the first stage of a real-world attack scenario. If an attacker finds a weakness in an exposed system, it could serve as the entry point for further exploitation. This makes external assessments vital for protecting the attack surface that is visible to the world. For example, a vulnerability in a publicly available content management system or a misconfigured cloud storage bucket can lead to data breaches if left unaddressed. External assessments not only reveal technical flaws but also expose policy gaps, such as failure to decommission outdated services or neglecting to implement multifactor authentication on critical endpoints.

Internal vulnerability assessments, on the other hand, are conducted from within the organization's trusted environment. These assessments simulate what an attacker could do after breaching the external defenses or what an insider with malicious intent or compromised credentials might access. Internal assessments examine systems such as workstations, internal application servers, file shares, databases, and network devices. The objective is to identify vulnerabilities that could enable privilege escalation, lateral movement, data exfiltration, or service disruption within the internal network.

One of the key reasons internal assessments are essential is because breaches are not always prevented at the perimeter. Once an attacker is inside the network, whether through phishing, stolen credentials, or a third-party compromise, the focus shifts from keeping them out to limiting what they can do. Internal assessments help identify weak passwords, unpatched systems, overly permissive access controls, and systems that lack proper segmentation. These weaknesses are often overlooked because they are not directly exposed to the outside world, but they can significantly impact the speed and scope of a compromise once an intruder is inside.

Another important consideration is that internal assessments can reveal issues introduced by day-to-day operations. As environments grow, changes to configurations, software deployments, and administrative practices can lead to unintended exposures. For example, a developer might temporarily disable security settings for testing and forget to re-enable them, or a file share might be accessible to all domain users due to misconfigured permissions. Internal scans provide visibility into these operational flaws before they can be exploited.

Frequency and scope also differ between internal and external assessments. External assessments are often performed on a scheduled basis, such as monthly or quarterly, especially for regulatory compliance. Internal assessments may be more frequent, even continuous, depending on the risk appetite and resources of the organization. Both types should be performed after major infrastructure changes or new application deployments. The scope of an internal assessment is typically broader because it includes a larger number of systems, whereas external assessments are limited to publicly accessible infrastructure.

Technology used in these assessments often overlaps but may be configured differently. External assessments prioritize stealth and minimal disruption, using safe scanning techniques to avoid drawing attention or triggering denial of service. Internal assessments may be more aggressive and thorough, scanning deeper into system configurations and registry settings. Tools used include commercial vulnerability scanners, open-source solutions, and customized scripts tailored to the specific environment. However, both assessments require skilled interpretation to separate false positives from actionable findings and to contextualize risks based on asset criticality and exposure.

The outputs of internal and external assessments feed into the broader vulnerability management lifecycle. Detected vulnerabilities must be evaluated for risk, prioritized for remediation, and assigned to the appropriate teams for action. External findings often take priority due to their visibility and exploitation potential, but internal findings should not be underestimated, particularly those involving sensitive systems or high-privilege access. The effectiveness of remediation efforts must be validated through follow-up scans, and unresolved vulnerabilities should be tracked and reported until addressed or accepted through risk exceptions.

Integrating both internal and external vulnerability assessments into a single program ensures that no blind spots exist. The external view keeps the organization alert to outside threats, while the internal view focuses on minimizing damage from breaches that bypass or defeat external defenses. The convergence of these perspectives leads to a more resilient security posture. It enables the organization to defend against a broader range of attack vectors and to build a defense-in-depth strategy that anticipates, contains, and recovers from incidents more effectively.

Communication and coordination between teams conducting internal and external assessments are also crucial. In some organizations, these assessments are handled by separate departments or even outsourced to third parties. Without proper integration, the insights from each assessment may not be fully leveraged, and duplicated efforts or gaps in coverage may occur. Establishing a centralized vulnerability management team or function helps ensure that findings are consistently evaluated, prioritized, and remediated, regardless of their source. It also promotes a unified approach to risk management, where both external exposure and internal weaknesses are considered in strategic planning and resource allocation.

Internal and external vulnerability assessments are not optional but foundational. They offer complementary views of the same problem and work best when executed in concert. In a world of constantly evolving threats, relying on only one type of assessment creates a false sense of security. Organizations must look outward to guard against external attackers and look inward to detect and correct weaknesses that could be exploited from within. The most secure enterprises are those that continuously evaluate both perspectives, use the insights to drive improvement, and treat vulnerability management as a dynamic, ongoing process that adapts to the changing digital landscape.

Mobile Device Vulnerability Management

Mobile device vulnerability management has emerged as one of the most important and challenging areas in modern cybersecurity. As smartphones, tablets, and other mobile devices become integral to business operations, they introduce a wide range of risks that organizations must address proactively. These devices are no longer used solely for communication. They provide access to corporate email, cloud applications, internal systems, and sensitive data. They also frequently operate outside the traditional security perimeter, connecting to public Wi-Fi networks, using third-party applications, and storing data locally. The combination of mobility, access, and functionality makes them high-value targets for attackers and requires a dedicated approach to identifying and managing their vulnerabilities.

The first challenge in mobile device vulnerability management is visibility. Unlike traditional workstations and servers, mobile devices are often personally owned, sporadically connected to the corporate network, and subject to varying degrees of control. This makes it difficult for security teams to maintain an accurate inventory of all devices accessing corporate resources. Mobile device management solutions and enterprise mobility management platforms play a critical role in addressing this challenge by providing a centralized interface for tracking devices, enforcing policies, and monitoring activity. These tools enable organizations to identify devices that are jailbroken or rooted, running outdated operating systems, or using insecure applications. Without this visibility, vulnerabilities can go unnoticed, leaving the organization exposed.

Operating system vulnerabilities on mobile devices are a primary concern. Both Android and iOS regularly release updates to patch security flaws, some of which are severe and could allow remote code execution, privilege escalation, or unauthorized access to device features. However, the fragmented nature of the Android ecosystem, in particular, means that many devices do not receive timely updates.

Some manufacturers delay or entirely skip updates, leaving users dependent on outdated software. Even in enterprise environments, users may postpone updates for convenience or compatibility reasons. This delay creates a significant window of opportunity for attackers who can exploit known vulnerabilities before they are patched. Organizations must implement policies that require users to maintain up-to-date systems and may need to restrict access to corporate resources for non-compliant devices.

Application vulnerabilities are another critical area. Mobile devices often have dozens or even hundreds of installed applications, many of which request broad permissions and access to sensitive data. Vulnerabilities in these applications, whether due to insecure coding practices, poor encryption, or lack of input validation, can serve as gateways for attackers. The use of mobile application management tools allows organizations to control which apps are installed, restrict access to corporate data, and enforce security policies on a per-app basis. Additionally, mobile threat defense solutions can analyze application behavior and detect suspicious or malicious activity, providing an added layer of protection against vulnerabilities introduced through third-party software.

The threat of malicious applications is amplified by the presence of unofficial app stores and side-loaded apps, especially on Android devices. Users who install apps from untrusted sources may inadvertently introduce malware that exploits device vulnerabilities or exfiltrates data. Organizations must take steps to educate users about the risks of unapproved apps and enforce technical controls that block installation from unknown sources. App whitelisting, along with network monitoring, helps ensure that only trusted applications are running on enterprise-connected devices and that any attempts to bypass these controls are flagged for investigation.

Network vulnerabilities are also a concern for mobile devices, particularly because they frequently connect to unsecured or public Wi-Fi networks. These connections can be exploited by attackers to perform man-in-the-middle attacks, intercept traffic, or distribute malware. Virtual private network solutions are essential for securing mobile traffic and ensuring that sensitive communications are encrypted, even over untrusted networks. Some organizations choose to route all mobile traffic through VPN gateways or cloud-based secure web gateways that can inspect traffic, apply filtering policies, and detect malicious behavior. These measures help reduce the risk of network-based attacks on mobile devices and ensure that security policies are consistently applied regardless of location.

Another critical consideration in mobile device vulnerability management is data protection. Mobile devices are susceptible to loss or theft, which poses a significant risk if sensitive data is stored locally without adequate encryption or access control. Full-disk encryption, biometric authentication, and remote wipe capabilities are essential tools for minimizing the impact of a lost or stolen device. Organizations must also implement data leakage prevention strategies that restrict the ability to copy, share, or store corporate data outside of approved applications and environments. This includes separating personal and business data through containerization or using sandboxed environments to ensure that corporate data is isolated and protected from personal applications.

Email and messaging platforms on mobile devices are common vectors for phishing attacks and social engineering. Attackers craft messages that appear legitimate, using them to trick users into clicking malicious links, downloading infected attachments, or divulging credentials. These attacks may bypass traditional email filters, especially if users are accessing personal accounts or using third-party messaging apps. Mobile-specific phishing detection tools, user awareness training, and integration with enterprise security information and event management systems can help detect and mitigate these threats. Monitoring mobile device behavior and correlating it with known phishing campaigns enables faster response and better protection of users and data.

Integration between mobile security tools and broader enterprise security architecture is necessary to create a cohesive defense strategy. Mobile threat intelligence must feed into central monitoring systems, enabling security teams to correlate mobile incidents with other events and detect broader attack campaigns. Policies governing mobile device usage must align with overall access control frameworks, and any vulnerabilities identified on mobile platforms must be incorporated into the organization's overall vulnerability management lifecycle. This includes tracking vulnerabilities from discovery to remediation, documenting exceptions, and performing post-remediation validation.

As the use of mobile devices continues to grow and become more integral to business operations, the risks associated with mobile vulnerabilities will increase. Organizations must adapt by treating mobile devices as fully fledged endpoints that require the same level of security scrutiny as desktops and servers. This includes proactive scanning, timely patching, behavioral monitoring, and consistent enforcement of security policies. Mobile device vulnerability management is no longer a secondary concern but a primary pillar of enterprise security. Failure to address it not only exposes sensitive data and systems but also undermines the trust and agility that mobile technology was meant to provide. A mature mobile security program is essential to ensure that convenience does not come at the cost of compromise.

Patch Testing and Change Control

Patch testing and change control are essential components of any mature vulnerability management program. They represent the structured, deliberate processes that ensure changes to systems, particularly those intended to remediate security vulnerabilities, do not introduce new risks, disrupt services, or create unintended consequences. While applying patches may seem like a straightforward activity, especially given the frequency of updates issued by software vendors, the reality is far more complex in enterprise environments. These environments are made up of diverse systems, interconnected applications, and legacy dependencies, all of which must be considered carefully before changes are implemented. Failing to follow a disciplined approach to patch testing and change control can result in system outages, degraded performance, security regression, or worse, the introduction of new attack vectors.

Patch testing is the first line of defense against these unintended outcomes. Before deploying a patch in a production environment, it must be tested thoroughly in a controlled setting that mirrors the production configuration as closely as possible. This testing process typically begins with the installation of the patch in a staging or quality assurance environment. The patch is then evaluated not only for successful installation but also for its impact on system functionality, application compatibility, and performance. Test cases are run to verify that critical business processes continue to function as expected, and that the patch does not interfere with integrations or dependent services. This process is particularly important when patches affect operating systems, middleware, or software platforms that host mission-critical applications.

In some cases, patch testing reveals issues that would not have been apparent without such scrutiny. For example, a security patch for a database server might inadvertently break an internal reporting tool that depends on a deprecated function. Or a patch for a web application framework might introduce latency that affects user experience. These risks are not theoretical; they are observed frequently in large-scale environments. As such, testing is not just a quality assurance measure, it is a risk mitigation strategy that prevents remediation efforts from becoming sources of instability or even additional vulnerabilities. Moreover, testing builds confidence across the organization, particularly among IT operations, development teams, and business stakeholders who rely on system availability and performance.

Change control is the framework that governs how patches and other modifications are approved, documented, scheduled, and implemented across an organization. It ensures that changes are made in a consistent, transparent, and auditable manner. Change control begins with the identification of a required update, often triggered by a vulnerability assessment, vendor advisory, or internal security review. Once a patch has been identified and tested, a change request is created and submitted to a formal change management board or system. This request includes detailed information about the patch, the systems it affects, the testing performed, the implementation plan, and a rollback strategy in case the update causes issues.

The change control board or designated approvers evaluate the request based on its risk, urgency, and potential impact. Emergency patches for zero-day vulnerabilities may be fast-tracked, but even these must follow a defined emergency change process. Routine updates are scheduled according to maintenance windows and operational considerations, such as avoiding peak usage periods or aligning with other planned updates. Documentation is maintained at every step, capturing the rationale for the change, the personnel involved, the execution timeline, and the outcome. This documentation is not only useful for future reference but also necessary for compliance with industry regulations and standards that require change control evidence during audits.

Another critical aspect of change control is communication. Stakeholders must be informed about upcoming changes, particularly when they may affect system availability or functionality. Effective communication includes notifying users, coordinating with application owners, and ensuring that support teams are prepared to handle issues if they arise. This transparency reduces resistance to changes, builds trust in the process, and facilitates collaboration across departments. When communication is neglected, even successful patches can cause disruption simply because users were unprepared or unaware of temporary changes in system behavior.

The rollback or back-out plan is a safety net that allows changes to be reversed if they lead to unforeseen problems. Every patch implementation plan must include a clearly defined rollback strategy, with documented procedures for restoring systems to their previous state. This often involves creating full system backups or snapshots prior to applying the patch, so that recovery can be performed quickly and with minimal data loss. Rollbacks are especially important in high-availability environments where downtime can have significant financial or operational consequences. The ability to reverse a change not only protects the business but also gives teams the confidence to proceed with patching more regularly and efficiently.

Automation is becoming increasingly important in both patch testing and change control. Automated testing tools can accelerate validation by executing predefined test cases, comparing performance metrics, and identifying regressions. Similarly, automated change management platforms can streamline the creation, tracking, and approval of change requests, while also integrating with configuration management and deployment tools to enforce consistency. Automation reduces human error, speeds up response times, and enhances visibility into the change process. However, automation must be implemented thoughtfully, with safeguards that prevent unintended changes and provide alerts when anomalies are detected.

The coordination between vulnerability management, patch testing, and change control must be seamless. A vulnerability cannot be considered remediated until the patch is not only installed but also tested, approved, and verified in production. This interconnected process ensures that security improvements do not come at the expense of operational stability. It also reinforces a culture of shared responsibility, where security, IT, and business teams collaborate to protect the organization while maintaining performance and reliability.

In complex environments, the lack of proper patch testing and change control can turn routine updates into high-risk activities. Conversely, when these processes are well-defined, practiced, and continuously improved, they become enablers of agility and resilience. Organizations can respond to threats faster, with greater confidence, and with fewer negative consequences. They can maintain compliance with regulatory frameworks, build trust with stakeholders, and support digital transformation efforts without compromising security. Patch testing and change control are not merely operational tasks; they are strategic functions that enable secure and stable growth in an increasingly dynamic and hostile cyber landscape.

Remediation Timeframes and SLAs

Remediation timeframes and service level agreements play a foundational role in the effectiveness and maturity of any vulnerability management program. They define how quickly identified vulnerabilities must be addressed based on their severity, risk to the business, and potential exposure to threats. Without clearly defined timeframes and enforcement mechanisms, vulnerabilities can remain unaddressed indefinitely, increasing the likelihood of successful exploitation and breach. On the other hand, setting unrealistic expectations or rigid timelines that do not align with operational realities can cause friction between security and IT teams, ultimately undermining the entire vulnerability management process. Achieving the right balance requires a strategic approach that considers both the urgency of the threat and the organization's capacity to respond.

At the heart of remediation timeframes is the concept of prioritization. Not all vulnerabilities pose the same level of risk, and therefore they should not be remediated on the same schedule. Critical vulnerabilities, especially those with known exploits in the wild or affecting internet-facing systems, require immediate attention. In many organizations, the SLA for these types of vulnerabilities is set between twenty-four and seventy-two hours, depending on the potential impact and exploitability. High-risk vulnerabilities, while not necessarily exploitable immediately, still demand timely remediation, often within a seven-day window. Medium and low-risk vulnerabilities are usually addressed within thirty to ninety days, unless specific conditions elevate their risk profile.

These timeframes are often codified into service level agreements that define the expectations for how quickly vulnerabilities must be triaged, remediated, and verified. SLAs are formal commitments, typically documented in organizational policies or contracts, and are used to hold teams accountable. They serve as benchmarks for performance and are commonly reviewed during audits, compliance assessments, and risk management evaluations. An SLA is not just a technical guideline; it is a governance tool that aligns security objectives with operational responsibilities. It creates a shared understanding between security teams, system owners, and business units about what is expected and what timelines must be respected.

Enforcing SLAs requires reliable measurement and reporting. Vulnerability management tools must be configured to track the time of vulnerability discovery, the assignment of remediation tasks, the implementation of patches or mitigations, and the verification of resolution. Dashboards and reports should provide real-time insights into SLA compliance, highlighting overdue items, trends over time, and recurring issues. These reports are essential not only for internal monitoring but also for demonstrating compliance with industry regulations such as PCI DSS, HIPAA, and ISO 27001, all of which emphasize the importance of timely remediation. They also support communication with stakeholders who may not be involved in daily remediation efforts but need assurance that risks are being managed effectively.

While SLAs are critical, they must be designed with flexibility. There will be legitimate cases where remediation within the SLA timeframe is not feasible due to technical constraints, business dependencies, or the potential for disruption. For example, patching a critical vulnerability on a production database may require downtime that is incompatible with current business needs. In such cases, organizations should have a defined process for exception management. This process involves formally documenting the reason for the delay, assessing the residual risk, and implementing compensating controls such as network segmentation, monitoring, or temporary configuration changes. Exceptions should be reviewed and approved by security and business leadership and revisited regularly to ensure they remain justified.

Another important consideration in setting SLAs is the availability of resources. Security and IT teams are often under pressure to manage large volumes of vulnerabilities across diverse systems with limited personnel. Automation can help by streamlining the detection, prioritization, and remediation workflows. However, even with automation, organizations must realistically assess what can be accomplished within the specified timeframes. Overly aggressive SLAs can lead to burnout, rushed changes that introduce new risks, or superficial fixes that do not address the root cause. By involving operational teams in the creation of SLAs, organizations can ensure that expectations are achievable and that teams are committed to meeting them.

The dynamic nature of threat landscapes also affects how SLAs are applied. A vulnerability that appears low-risk today may become critical tomorrow if new exploit code is released or if threat actors begin actively targeting it. SLAs must be flexible enough to accommodate these changes, allowing for reprioritization based on updated threat intelligence. Integration between threat intelligence platforms and vulnerability management systems can automate this process, ensuring that the most dangerous vulnerabilities rise to the top of the queue. This adaptive approach allows organizations to remain responsive without overburdening their remediation teams.

Communication is vital to the success of SLA enforcement. Teams must be informed not only about what vulnerabilities exist but also about why specific deadlines are in place and what the potential consequences of delays are. Clear communication fosters accountability and enables collaboration between security, operations, and application owners. Regular review meetings, shared dashboards, and escalation paths for SLA violations help keep everyone aligned and responsive. When SLAs are missed, the goal should be to understand why, learn from the failure, and refine processes to prevent recurrence.

SLAs also serve as a benchmark for continuous improvement. Over time, organizations should analyze their SLA performance to identify bottlenecks, recurring challenges, and opportunities for optimization. For example, if critical vulnerabilities are consistently being remediated late, it may indicate a need for better patch management tools, more cross-functional coordination, or additional training. If certain teams or systems repeatedly fall short, targeted interventions can be implemented. On the other hand, high levels of SLA compliance can be celebrated and used to build a culture of security excellence.

Ultimately, remediation timeframes and SLAs are about accountability, transparency, and risk reduction. They bring structure to vulnerability management, ensure timely response to security threats, and align technical actions with organizational priorities. When implemented thoughtfully and monitored consistently, they become a powerful force for resilience and a clear signal that the organization takes cybersecurity seriously. They provide measurable, actionable goals for security teams and a clear standard of care that supports trust, compliance, and long-term operational integrity.

Training and Awareness for IT Teams

Training and awareness for IT teams are essential components of an effective vulnerability management strategy. The evolving threat landscape, the increasing complexity of technology environments, and the growing sophistication of attackers require that IT personnel remain continuously educated, alert, and prepared to respond to security issues. Vulnerability management is not only a technical process involving tools and automation but also a human-driven discipline that depends on the knowledge, judgment, and coordination of the people responsible for implementing and maintaining secure systems. A well-trained IT team can recognize risks early, act decisively to mitigate them, and contribute to a culture of security that extends beyond any one department or toolset.

One of the foundational reasons for investing in training is the pace at which vulnerabilities emerge. New vulnerabilities are discovered daily, often with far-reaching implications. IT teams are expected to identify these vulnerabilities quickly, understand their impact, prioritize them correctly, and apply appropriate remediation steps. Without a strong understanding of security principles, operating system internals, application behavior, and networking fundamentals, teams may struggle to distinguish between low-priority flaws and critical vulnerabilities that could be exploited within hours. Training helps IT professionals interpret vulnerability reports accurately, understand the context behind severity scores, and take informed actions that reduce risk rather than simply meeting compliance checkboxes.

Awareness training also ensures that IT personnel are aligned with current organizational policies, regulatory requirements, and industry best practices. Regulations such as GDPR, HIPAA, PCI DSS, and others often include specific mandates around patch management, configuration hardening, and access controls. Failing to comply can lead to legal consequences, financial penalties, and reputational damage. By keeping IT staff informed about these requirements and how they apply to their roles, organizations reduce the risk of accidental non-compliance. Training sessions can provide real-world examples, walkthroughs of audit findings, and lessons learned from past incidents to make the connection between policy and practice clear and actionable.

Another critical benefit of training is the reduction of human error. Many security incidents are not caused by complex, zero-day exploits but by simple misconfigurations, missed patches, or poor operational practices. A server left exposed to the internet, a default password left unchanged, or a firewall rule written too broadly can all result in serious breaches. When IT teams are properly trained, they are more likely to follow secure configuration guidelines, double-check their work, and understand the potential consequences of their decisions. This heightened sense of responsibility and attention to detail creates a safer environment and reduces the organization's overall attack surface.

Training should not be limited to static, one-time courses. The dynamic nature of technology and threats requires a continuous learning approach. This can include regular workshops, webinars, hands-on labs, and certifications that are updated to reflect the latest developments. In addition, tabletop exercises and red team/blue team simulations provide an opportunity for IT staff to experience security incidents in a controlled environment. These exercises teach not only technical skills but also coordination, communication, and crisis management. They highlight how vulnerabilities can be exploited, how attackers think, and what steps are effective in containment and remediation. The result is a team that is more resilient, more confident, and more capable of responding under pressure.

Cross-functional training is also crucial. IT teams do not work in isolation, and effective vulnerability management requires collaboration with security analysts, application developers, network engineers, and business stakeholders. Training programs should therefore include components that explain the roles and responsibilities of different teams, foster a shared vocabulary, and build an understanding of how individual actions impact broader organizational goals. For example, a developer may not need to be a security expert but should understand secure coding principles and the importance of addressing vulnerabilities flagged by static code analysis tools. Similarly, a network engineer should be aware of how segmentation and access controls can prevent the spread of malware within a compromised environment.

Management support is vital to the success of training and awareness efforts. Leaders must prioritize security education, allocate time for training activities, and recognize the importance of ongoing professional development. When IT staff are overloaded with operational duties and given no time to attend training or stay current with new threats, the organization ultimately suffers. Investing in training is an investment in organizational resilience, and management must communicate that security is a shared responsibility, not an afterthought or the sole domain of the security team.

Metrics can help assess the effectiveness of training initiatives. Organizations can track completion rates for required courses, measure knowledge retention through quizzes or assessments, and monitor improvements in incident response times or vulnerability remediation metrics over time. Surveys and feedback mechanisms can also provide insight into whether training is relevant, engaging, and applicable to the challenges teams face. These metrics not only inform future training content but also demonstrate to executives that education efforts are yielding tangible benefits.

Culture plays a significant role in sustaining awareness. A culture that values continuous improvement, encourages questions, and supports open discussions about security fosters better outcomes than one that relies on blame or fear. When team members feel safe admitting they need help or reporting a mistake, problems are addressed sooner and more constructively. Celebrating successful patch cycles, highlighting individuals who caught and corrected misconfigurations, or sharing stories of thwarted attacks can reinforce positive behaviors and show that security is woven into the fabric of the organization.

Finally, awareness must extend beyond the technical aspects of vulnerability management. IT teams should understand the broader business context of their work, including how vulnerabilities can impact customer trust, revenue, brand reputation, and strategic goals. When technical staff see how their actions contribute to the organization's success or failure, they are more likely to act with care and urgency. Framing security in business terms helps bridge the gap between IT and leadership and ensures that everyone is working toward the same objectives.

Training and awareness for IT teams are not optional add-ons to a security program; they are fundamental enablers of success. In an era where threats evolve rapidly and the cost of failure can be catastrophic, the human element remains both the most critical asset and the most exploitable weakness. By empowering IT personnel with the knowledge, tools, and mindset needed to manage vulnerabilities effectively, organizations strengthen their defenses, improve their agility, and foster a culture where security is everyone's responsibility.

Communication Across Departments

Effective communication across departments is a critical success factor in any vulnerability management program. In large and even mid-sized organizations, the responsibility for managing vulnerabilities does not fall on a single team. It involves coordination between security professionals, IT operations, software development teams, network administrators, compliance officers, business unit leaders, and sometimes even legal and human resources departments. Each of these groups brings a different perspective, a different set of priorities, and often a different vocabulary. Without strong interdepartmental communication, efforts to identify, assess, prioritize, and remediate vulnerabilities can become fragmented, delayed, or misaligned, leading to increased risk and potential exposure to attacks.

One of the key challenges in cross-departmental communication is aligning technical details with business objectives. Security teams typically speak in terms of CVEs, exploitability, severity scores, and threat actors, while business units focus on revenue impact, operational continuity, customer satisfaction, and regulatory compliance. Bridging this gap requires security leaders and vulnerability managers to translate technical findings into business-relevant language. Instead of simply stating that a critical vulnerability was found on a server, they must explain what that server does, what kind of data it handles, who relies on it, and what could happen if it were compromised. This contextual framing helps business leaders understand the urgency of remediation and allocate resources accordingly.

Equally important is the flow of information from business units to security teams. Security professionals may not have full visibility into how systems are used in practice, which applications are considered mission-critical, or what operational constraints exist that could delay patching or reconfiguration. Business units must communicate their priorities, upcoming changes, planned outages, and other factors that influence the feasibility and timing of remediation efforts. This dialogue helps security teams develop more realistic remediation plans and avoids disruptions to key business functions. It also fosters a sense of partnership, where security is seen as a supporter of business goals rather than a barrier to progress.

Timing and format of communication also matter. Vulnerability management is often a fast-moving domain, where new threats emerge suddenly and require rapid response. However, not all departments operate on the same cadence. While security may want to address a new vulnerability within twenty-four hours, the development team may already be in the middle of a release cycle, and the IT team may be operating under a strict change control window. Regular communication rhythms, such as weekly vulnerability review meetings, monthly risk management forums, and real-time alerting channels, can help ensure that all teams remain informed and aligned. These forums provide opportunities to discuss open issues, review upcoming patches, coordinate testing, and escalate high-priority concerns.

Centralized platforms for communication and tracking also support collaboration. Using shared tools such as ticketing systems, dashboards, and vulnerability management platforms allows all stakeholders to view the same information, track progress, and update statuses in real time. When security teams open remediation tickets, the IT team should see not only the technical details but also the risk context, remediation deadline, and recommended action. Similarly, when IT resolves a vulnerability or encounters a roadblock, that information should be visible to the security team and, when relevant, to business leadership. Transparent workflows reduce misunderstandings, minimize duplication of effort, and accelerate response times.

Escalation paths are a critical component of effective communication. Not all issues can be resolved at the operational level. Some remediation efforts may require exceptions, resource reallocation, or temporary acceptance of risk. In such cases, there must be a clear and documented process for escalating decisions to the appropriate level of authority. This might involve department heads, the risk management committee, or the chief information security officer. Escalations should be treated not as failures of the process but as a necessary part of making informed trade-offs between risk and business continuity. By handling these escalations transparently and collaboratively, organizations can maintain momentum while preserving accountability.

Culture also plays a significant role in shaping communication. In organizations where departments operate in silos, where blame is assigned instead of collaboration encouraged, communication around vulnerabilities often breaks down. Security teams may feel ignored, IT teams may feel overwhelmed, and business leaders may feel uninformed. In contrast, organizations that foster a culture of shared responsibility, where security is integrated into everyday operations and where open dialogue is encouraged, tend to manage vulnerabilities more effectively. Creating this culture requires leadership support, cross-functional training, and recognition of the contributions that each department makes to the organization's security posture.

Training and awareness programs can also help improve communication. When developers understand the basics of secure coding and vulnerability management, they are more receptive to feedback from security teams and more capable of addressing findings quickly. When business leaders receive briefings on current threats and risk trends, they are more likely to support proactive investments in security. And when IT operations staff participate in incident response exercises or tabletop scenarios, they gain a better understanding of how their actions influence broader organizational outcomes. Education builds empathy, common ground, and a shared vocabulary that improves every interaction.

Ultimately, communication across departments ensures that vulnerability management is not just a security function but an enterprise-wide discipline. It aligns the efforts of multiple teams toward a common goal, enables informed decision-making, and ensures that risks are addressed efficiently and effectively. In today's interconnected digital environments, where threats evolve rapidly and attackers exploit gaps in visibility and coordination, strong communication is as critical as any technical control. It allows organizations to act with speed, clarity, and purpose, protecting their assets, their reputation, and their future.

Strategic Planning for Vulnerability Reduction

Strategic planning for vulnerability reduction involves a deliberate, long-term approach to minimizing the number, impact, and exploitability of vulnerabilities across an organization's infrastructure. Unlike reactive vulnerability management, which focuses on responding to threats as they arise, strategic planning aims to create a proactive environment where security is built into processes, systems are designed to resist exploitation, and the organization moves toward a sustainable reduction in risk over time. This approach requires the integration of technical controls, organizational governance, and cultural change to shift from firefighting mode into a state of controlled and measurable improvement.

The first step in strategic planning is understanding the current landscape. This includes a comprehensive inventory of assets, including hardware, software, cloud services, and network segments. Without a clear understanding of what exists within the organization, it is impossible to secure it effectively. Strategic planning requires not just identification of assets, but also classification based on business criticality, data sensitivity, and exposure to external threats. This contextual information helps prioritize resources and ensures that efforts are focused where they matter most. Once the environment is mapped, the organization must assess its vulnerability profile by analyzing historical data on recurring vulnerabilities, common misconfigurations, patching delays, and areas of frequent non-compliance.

From this baseline, organizations can begin to define strategic goals. These goals should be aligned with the broader mission of the organization and reflect realistic improvements based on current capabilities and resources. For example, a strategic objective might be to reduce the average time to remediate critical vulnerabilities by fifty percent within twelve months. Another goal could be to increase patching compliance on high-value systems to ninety-eight percent. These targets must be specific, measurable, achievable, relevant, and time-bound. Setting clear goals creates accountability and provides a foundation for tracking progress. It also communicates the organization's commitment to security to both internal and external stakeholders.

One of the core pillars of strategic vulnerability reduction is investment in automation and tooling. Manual processes are slow, error-prone, and difficult to scale in complex environments. By automating asset discovery, vulnerability scanning, patch deployment, and reporting, organizations can reduce operational overhead and free up skilled personnel to focus on strategic initiatives. Automation also enables more frequent assessments and quicker responses to new vulnerabilities. However, implementing tools is not sufficient on its own. Strategic planning must include the evaluation and integration of these tools into existing workflows, ensuring that they enhance rather than complicate the vulnerability management process.

Another essential aspect of strategic planning is the development of standardized processes and policies. When vulnerability management activities are ad hoc or left to individual teams, consistency suffers, and gaps inevitably emerge. A strategic approach requires the creation of policies that define how vulnerabilities are identified, evaluated, prioritized, and remediated. These policies should be enforced through governance structures that include regular audits, exception handling procedures, and escalation paths. Standardization ensures that every vulnerability is treated according to its risk, not based on who discovered it or which team owns the system. It also enables cross-functional collaboration and simplifies training, reporting, and compliance efforts.

People and culture play a central role in strategic vulnerability reduction. A plan is only as strong as the people who execute it, and security cannot be effective in an organization where it is treated as a low priority or the responsibility of a single team. Strategic planning must include efforts to build a culture of shared responsibility, where security is integrated into every role and department. This involves regular training for IT teams, developers, and business units, as well as clear communication about why vulnerability reduction matters and how it supports the organization's mission. Recognizing and rewarding good security practices reinforces positive behavior and helps drive long-term change.

Strategic planning must also address legacy systems and technical debt. In many organizations, older systems persist because they support critical functions or because replacing them is expensive or disruptive. However, these systems often lack modern security controls and are difficult or impossible to patch. A strategic approach includes developing roadmaps for phasing out or isolating legacy systems. This might involve migrating to modern platforms, segmenting networks, implementing compensating controls, or using virtualization to limit exposure. Addressing technical debt is one of the most challenging but necessary parts of reducing long-term vulnerability.

Measurement and metrics are critical to strategic planning. Organizations must continuously monitor their progress toward defined goals, using key performance indicators to assess effectiveness and identify areas for improvement. These indicators may include metrics such as mean time to remediation, percentage of systems scanned within a given timeframe, number of critical vulnerabilities per asset type, and rate of patch failures. Metrics should be reported at multiple levels, from technical dashboards for operational teams to executive summaries for senior leadership. Transparent reporting helps maintain momentum, secures continued investment, and ensures that strategic initiatives remain aligned with business objectives.

Finally, strategic vulnerability reduction must be resilient and adaptable. Threat landscapes evolve, technologies change, and organizational priorities shift. A rigid plan that cannot adapt to new conditions will quickly become obsolete. Strategic planning should be revisited regularly, with quarterly or annual reviews that assess progress, incorporate lessons learned, and adjust goals as needed. Feedback loops from incident response, threat intelligence, and penetration testing should be used to refine the strategy continuously. By embedding agility into the planning process, organizations can ensure that their vulnerability reduction efforts remain relevant and effective in a dynamic world.

Strategic planning for vulnerability reduction transforms security from a reactive necessity into a proactive capability. It aligns technical efforts with organizational goals, reduces exposure to cyber threats, and creates a foundation for sustainable improvement. Through careful analysis, thoughtful investment, and cross-functional collaboration, organizations can move beyond merely managing vulnerabilities and begin reducing them in a measurable and meaningful way. This shift not only strengthens security but also enhances resilience, builds trust, and supports innovation in an increasingly connected and complex digital environment.

Measuring Program Maturity

Measuring program maturity in the context of vulnerability management is essential for understanding how effective an organization's efforts are in identifying, prioritizing, and remediating vulnerabilities across its infrastructure. Maturity is not a static measure but a continuum that reflects how well processes, technologies, and people are integrated and optimized to reduce risk. A mature program is proactive rather than reactive, integrated rather than siloed, and consistent rather than ad hoc. It reflects an organization's ability not only to react to threats efficiently but also to anticipate them, minimize exposure, and build long-term resilience. Measuring maturity helps identify strengths and weaknesses, set goals, justify investments, and benchmark progress over time or against peers within an industry.

The foundation of maturity measurement begins with the establishment of a structured framework. Common models used to assess vulnerability management maturity include the Capability Maturity Model Integration and NIST's Cybersecurity Framework. These models provide a tiered approach that ranges from informal, ad hoc practices to optimized, automated, and continuously improving processes. At the lowest levels of maturity, organizations may lack visibility into their assets, have no formal patching process, and respond to vulnerabilities only after a security incident has occurred. As maturity increases, the organization begins to implement formal procedures, measure performance, and eventually adopt a data-driven, risk-based approach that enables rapid and consistent remediation across all systems.

A key element in measuring maturity is evaluating the consistency of practices across departments and environments. In an immature program, different business units may follow their own procedures for patching and remediation, resulting in duplicated efforts, conflicting priorities, and uneven risk exposure. A mature program ensures that vulnerability management is standardized through organization-wide policies, documented processes, and centralized governance. This includes defining roles and responsibilities for detection, analysis, prioritization, remediation, and validation. The ability to consistently apply policies across cloud environments, on-premise systems, remote devices, and third-party platforms is a strong indicator of program maturity.

Asset visibility is another core component of maturity. Organizations cannot protect what they cannot see, and comprehensive asset inventories are critical for effective vulnerability management. Maturity in this area is measured by the organization's ability to maintain real-time, accurate inventories of all hardware and software assets. This includes discovering shadow IT, tracking devices across dynamic environments, and ensuring that each asset is tagged with relevant context such as owner, location, criticality, and exposure. Mature programs integrate asset management with vulnerability scanning tools, configuration management databases, and access control systems to create a unified view of the attack surface.

Prioritization capabilities are central to understanding maturity. Immature programs may treat all vulnerabilities equally, leading to inefficient use of resources and delayed remediation of high-risk issues. A mature program employs contextual risk-based prioritization that considers factors such as asset value, exploitability, threat intelligence, and business impact. The use of scoring systems like CVSS is augmented with internal risk models and input from threat intelligence feeds to dynamically adjust priorities. The integration of vulnerability data with SIEM platforms and threat analytics further enhances the ability to focus on the vulnerabilities that matter most. The organization's ability to adapt its prioritization in response to emerging threats, rather than relying on static severity scores, reflects higher levels of maturity.

Remediation effectiveness is another critical measure. Mature programs track how quickly vulnerabilities are resolved based on their severity and risk. Metrics such as mean time to remediate, percentage of vulnerabilities closed within SLA, and rate of patch failures provide insight into the efficiency of the remediation process. Beyond speed, maturity also involves evaluating the thoroughness and reliability of remediation. This includes testing patches before deployment, validating that fixes were successful, and ensuring that no systems were missed during patch cycles. The presence of rollback procedures, change control, and coordination with IT and business units demonstrates a mature and disciplined approach.

Automation is both a sign and a driver of maturity. As organizations grow in complexity, manual processes become unsustainable. Mature programs leverage automation for asset discovery, vulnerability scanning, ticket generation, patch deployment, and reporting. Automation reduces the likelihood of human error, accelerates response times, and frees up skilled personnel to focus on strategic tasks. Measuring the extent to which key tasks are automated, and the reliability of those automated workflows, provides a tangible indicator of maturity. However, automation alone is not enough. Mature organizations also ensure that automated processes are continuously monitored, tested, and improved.

Another area to evaluate is integration. Maturity increases as vulnerability management becomes integrated with other cybersecurity and IT processes. This includes connections with incident response, configuration management, identity and access management, compliance tracking, and procurement. For example, if a new vulnerability is detected during an incident investigation, the ability to cross-reference it with vulnerability scans and patch history accelerates containment and root cause analysis. Integration with procurement ensures that newly acquired systems or software are vetted for security before deployment. The seamless flow of information between tools and teams reduces silos and ensures that security is embedded in all phases of the asset lifecycle.

Maturity can also be measured through cultural indicators. A mature program is supported by a culture where security is viewed as a shared responsibility. This is evident when IT teams embrace vulnerability remediation as part of routine maintenance, developers prioritize security in the SDLC, and executives understand and support vulnerability risk reduction as a business objective. Training participation, adherence to policies, and the willingness to report issues are all signs of a healthy security culture. Regular communication, awareness campaigns, and leadership engagement are essential to building and sustaining this culture.

Finally, measurement of maturity must include continuous improvement. A mature organization regularly reviews its vulnerability management practices, updates policies, audits outcomes, and adapts to new technologies and threats. It sets measurable goals, tracks progress, and learns from incidents and near misses. This commitment to improvement distinguishes mature programs from those that stagnate or regress. The presence of feedback loops, post-remediation reviews, and structured lessons learned sessions provides evidence that the organization is not just managing vulnerabilities but evolving in its ability to reduce them over time.

Measuring program maturity is not about achieving perfection but about understanding where the organization stands and what steps are needed to progress. It provides clarity, drives accountability, and enables smarter decisions. By assessing capabilities across people, processes, and technology, organizations can chart a path toward greater resilience, more efficient operations, and a stronger security posture. In a world where cyber threats are constant and evolving, maturity is not a luxury but a necessity for sustainable risk management.

Continuous Improvement and Future Trends

Continuous improvement is the backbone of a resilient and adaptive vulnerability management program. In a digital world where threat landscapes shift rapidly and technology evolves at an unprecedented pace, maintaining security is not a destination but a dynamic process. Organizations must commit to ongoing refinement of their tools, processes, policies, and skills to remain one step ahead of attackers. Continuous improvement is not only about correcting past mistakes but also about anticipating future challenges, identifying inefficiencies, and seeking new opportunities to enhance security posture across all layers of the enterprise. A strong vulnerability management program must evolve beyond reactive response into a proactive and predictive capability that supports long-term risk reduction and operational excellence.

One of the core principles of continuous improvement is the practice of regular reviews and retrospectives. Security teams should conduct periodic assessments of their vulnerability management activities, asking critical questions about what went well, what could have been done better, and what changes are needed to improve outcomes. This involves reviewing incident data, remediation timelines, audit findings, and operational metrics such as mean time to remediate or SLA compliance rates. These insights are invaluable for identifying patterns and root causes. For example, if a particular type of vulnerability continues to recur across different systems, it may indicate a deeper issue with configuration baselines, third-party software, or developer training. By examining these recurring issues in a structured and honest way, organizations can make targeted improvements that deliver lasting results.

Automation plays a significant role in driving continuous improvement. As environments grow more complex and threats become more sophisticated, the ability to automate repetitive tasks, such as scanning, patching, and reporting, frees up valuable human resources and reduces the potential for error. Automation also enables consistency and speed, two key ingredients in maintaining strong security posture. However, automation must be continuously evaluated to ensure it is still effective. Scripts and playbooks should be audited, tools should be updated, and outcomes should be monitored to detect any failures or inefficiencies. Integrating artificial intelligence and machine learning into automation workflows is one of the most promising trends in this space, offering the ability to detect subtle anomalies, prioritize vulnerabilities more intelligently, and even predict future risks based on behavioral patterns and threat intelligence.

Another essential component of continuous improvement is feedback. Feedback should be gathered from all stakeholders involved in the vulnerability management lifecycle, including IT operations, development teams, business units, compliance officers, and end users. This feedback can highlight friction points, such as cumbersome approval processes, insufficient visibility into vulnerabilities, or unclear prioritization guidelines. Incorporating feedback into planning and decision-making ensures that security practices are aligned with operational realities and that teams are empowered rather than hindered by security requirements. Feedback loops also foster a sense of collaboration and shared ownership, which is critical for the sustainability of any security initiative.

The integration of vulnerability management with broader organizational goals is another area of opportunity for continuous improvement. Rather than treating security as an isolated function, mature organizations embed it into strategic planning, digital transformation initiatives, and product development cycles. Security becomes a value enabler, not a blocker. This alignment requires regular communication between security leaders and executive stakeholders, the use of business-relevant metrics, and a clear understanding of how vulnerability-related risks can impact customer trust, brand reputation, regulatory compliance, and operational continuity. Over time, this alignment helps elevate the importance of vulnerability management within the organization and secures the support needed to invest in people, processes, and technology.

Looking toward the future, several trends are likely to shape the next generation of vulnerability management practices. One of the most prominent is the rise of cloud-native and serverless architectures. As organizations continue to migrate workloads to the cloud, traditional models of vulnerability management must evolve. Cloud infrastructure is dynamic, ephemeral, and often managed through infrastructure as code. Security teams must adapt by adopting tools that provide continuous scanning of cloud configurations, container registries, and runtime environments. They must also work more closely with DevOps teams to integrate security checks into CI/CD pipelines and to enforce security policies through automated governance.

Another emerging trend is the use of real-time threat intelligence to drive contextual prioritization. Instead of relying solely on static severity scores, organizations are increasingly integrating live feeds of threat activity, adversary tactics, and exploit availability to dynamically assess which vulnerabilities pose the greatest risk at any given moment. This capability, often referred to as risk-based vulnerability management, allows security teams to focus on what is most likely to be exploited rather than what appears most severe on paper. As threat intelligence platforms become more advanced and accessible, the ability to correlate external risk signals with internal asset data will become a cornerstone of strategic defense.

The growing importance of digital supply chains and third-party risk management also requires a rethinking of vulnerability strategies. Organizations can no longer afford to focus exclusively on their internal systems. They must assess the security of vendors, partners, and open-source components that are deeply embedded in their operational ecosystems. This requires better visibility, stronger contractual requirements, and collaborative efforts to address vulnerabilities across organizational boundaries. The development of Software Bill of Materials standards and supply chain risk frameworks will play a key role in this evolution, helping organizations understand and manage the full scope of their exposure.

User education and awareness will continue to be a priority, particularly as attackers shift tactics toward social engineering and identity-based attacks. Even the most advanced vulnerability management program can be undermined if users fall victim to phishing or if access controls are poorly implemented. As such, continuous improvement must include investment in training, cultural engagement, and behavioral analytics. Organizations that prioritize the human element alongside technology will be better positioned to defend against a broad range of threats.

Finally, regulatory developments and industry standards will influence the direction of vulnerability management in the years to come. Governments and regulatory bodies are increasingly recognizing the importance of cybersecurity and imposing stricter requirements on organizations to identify and remediate vulnerabilities promptly. Compliance frameworks will evolve to include more granular expectations for vulnerability tracking, reporting, and validation. Organizations must stay informed about these changes and ensure that their programs are adaptable enough to meet both current and future obligations.

Continuous improvement is not a one-time effort but a mindset. It requires discipline, transparency, collaboration, and a willingness to challenge the status quo. By embracing this mindset and staying informed about future trends, organizations can build vulnerability management programs that are not only effective today but also resilient and forward-looking. In doing so, they create an environment where security supports innovation, sustains trust, and enables the organization to thrive in a world defined by constant change and digital risk.

www.ingramcontent.com/pod-product-compliance
Lightning Source LLC
LaVergne TN
LVHW051235050326
832903LV00028B/2418